The Question of When

The Question of When

A Practical Guide to Knowing When It's Time for Assisted Living, Memory Care, or Skilled Nursing

Cory Fosco

Campion Hall Press

Published by Campion Hall Press
Chicago, Illinois

Printed in the United States of America

First Edition, 2026

Print ISBN: 979-8-9952369-2-4
Ebook ISBN: 979-8-9952369-1-7

The information in this book is intended for general educational purposes only and does not constitute legal, financial, or medical advice. Readers should consult qualified professionals regarding their specific circumstances. Contact information for organizations listed in the appendices should be verified, as details may change.

For Cyndi, and for Fredo and Lily —

again, and always.

Contents

AUTHOR'S NOTE

Why I Finally Wrote This Book

I have wanted to write this book for more than twenty-five years. Over the decades, I would write a bit, doubt myself, set it down. Pick it back up, write some more, doubt myself again. Life moved forward — careers, a marriage, two children, and the book kept waiting. But I was always thinking about it, especially as people sought my advice. Friends and family kept calling. A parent who could no longer manage at home. A spouse whose memory had begun to slip. A sibling in crisis, a family that had no idea where to begin. They called because they knew I had spent my career in this world, and they needed someone to help them find their way through it. I always tried to help. And every time I did, I thought: this should be a book.

So here, finally, it is.

I want to tell you a little about where I come from, because I think it matters for understanding what kind of book this is and why I needed to write it.

When I graduated from Loyola University Chicago with a degree in creative writing, I had no clear plan for what came next.

What I did know, the thing I had always known, was that I wanted to serve people, and that I was drawn to older adults in a way I could not entirely explain. I applied to the Jesuit Volunteer Corps Southwest and was placed at the Mesa Senior Center in Arizona, working as an outreach worker with homebound seniors. My job was to help them access the services they needed — home delivered meals, housekeeping, shopping assistance, and to make sure no one fell through the cracks. It was there that I met a man named Steve Trahan, who became one of the most important mentors of my life. Steve taught me what it really meant to serve, not as a transaction, not as a program, but as a genuine commitment to the dignity and wellbeing of people who needed someone in their corner. I have carried that lesson into every job I have had since.

From the Mesa Senior Center, I was fortunate to find my way into skilled nursing. I worked as a social worker at a facility in South Phoenix, where a remarkable woman who ran the social services department took me under her wing and showed me how advocacy looks in a clinical setting — how to navigate systems on behalf of people who could not always navigate them alone. From there I moved to a second small facility, where I worked as Director of Social Services alongside nurses, aides, therapists, and every other member of a care team. I saw people at their most vulnerable. I saw care done beautifully and, sometimes, care done badly. I learned what made the difference. And I learned, in a way that has never left me, why advocacy matters — why having someone who knows the system and is willing to fight for you is not a luxury but a necessity.

It was also during those years, after my time at the Phoenix facilities, that something unexpected happened: I met my wife.

Cyndi and I had grown up a quarter mile apart, attended the same grammar school, the same junior high, the same high school, and somehow never really found each other until we crossed paths at a ManorCare facility in Libertyville, Illinois, where I was serving as Director of Admissions. We have been together ever since, and we have raised two children — Fredo and Lily, who are doing remarkable things with their lives and who remind me every day of what matters most. I tell this story not because it is charming (though I think it is), but because it captures something true about this industry: it is full of people who came to it because they cared, and who stayed because of the relationships they found there. I am one of them.

I would go on to hold Director of Admissions roles at two more ManorCare facilities before becoming a Market Development Representative, a progression that gave me an unusually complete picture of how families find their way to a care setting, what they need from the admission process, and how much the quality of that experience shapes everything that follows. I have always said that my years as a social worker and admissions director were among the best of my professional life, because I could feel, every day, that the work I was doing made a difference for real people in real moments of need.

I owe everything to this industry. That is not a figure of speech. It gave me my vocation, my education, my career, my wife, and the life we have built together. What I owe in return is the best I can give, and for over twenty-five years, I have believed that one of the things I could give was this book.

The families who come to me for guidance are not looking for theory. They are looking for someone who has been inside this world long enough to know how it actually works, the signals to watch for, the questions to ask, the conversations to have before they are forced upon you, the decisions that feel impossible but are, with the right information and the right framing, genuinely navigable. That is what I have tried to give them, one conversation at a time. This book is my attempt to give it to everyone else.

This is not a book about giving up. It is not a book about warehousing your loved one or abandoning your responsibilities as a son, daughter, or spouse. It is a book about love expressed through preparation — about giving the people you care for the best possible care, at the right time, in the right place, without the chaos and regret that come from deciding in crisis.

> *This industry is truly amazing. I have spent over three decades watching families navigate some of the hardest moments of their lives, and watching the people who work in long-term care show up for them with skill and compassion, day after day, in ways that rarely get the recognition they deserve. This book is for the families. But it is also, in some small way, a tribute to the people who do this work.*

A Note on the Stories in This Book

The families, caregivers, and situations described throughout these pages are not drawn from any single person or event. They are composites — built from thirty-four years of conversations with families facing one of the hardest decisions they will ever face, and from the perspectives of everyone I encountered along the way: nursing home owners and operators, clinicians, legal experts, financial teams, front-line nurses and aides, and the friends and family members who called me over the years because they didn't know who else to ask.

The details are real in the way that matters: the confusion, the grief, the rushed decisions, the things people wish someone had told them sooner. The people are not. Any resemblance to a specific individual is coincidental.

These stories belong to all of the families I have worked with over the years, not to any one of them.

INTRODUCTION

The Phone Call Nobody Is Ready For

SUNDAY AFTERNOON. A HOSPITAL WAITING ROOM.

The call came on a Sunday, the way these calls always seem to come.

Karen had been managing her father's life for two years. Not from a distance — managing it. She was the one who drove three hours every other weekend to check on him. The one who set up the pill organizer and then called mid-week to make sure he was using it. The one who quietly started paying his electric bill online after the second shutoff notice, and who'd had the same conversation about the car keys at least a dozen times without resolution. She noticed the refrigerator full of food, untouched. She noticed the same story told three times in a single conversation. She noticed, and she kept noticing, and she kept telling herself there was still time to figure out the next step.

She had not figured out the next step.

Now she was standing in the corridor of a hospital she'd never been to, in a city three hours from her home, while a doctor she'd never met explained that her 81-year-old father had fallen in the night, fractured his hip, and undergone emergency surgery that morning. He was stable. He was asking for her. And, the doctor said this gently, but he said it — her father could not go back to living alone.

Karen's brother flew in from Seattle. Her sister drove up from Charlotte. By Monday evening, the three of them were sitting in a conference room with a hospital social worker who was kind, clearly overworked, and carrying a clipboard.

> *"We have to discharge him by Wednesday or Thursday at the latest," the social worker said. "I can give you a list of skilled nursing facilities in the area that have available beds."*

Wednesday or Thursday. It was Monday evening.

In the space of 72 hours, Karen and her siblings would need to choose a place where their father might spend the rest of his life. Two years of managing his world from a distance, and none of it — none of the pill organizers, the phone calls, the weekend drives — had prepared her for this moment. They had no idea what questions to ask. They had no idea what Medicare would cover or for how long. They didn't know what a skilled nursing facility actually was, or how it differed from assisted living, or whether their father might eventually be able to go somewhere else. They didn't know how to evaluate the facilities on the list, what the staffing ratios meant, or what the five-star ratings on the Medicare website actually measured.

They chose the facility closest to Karen's house. It had a nice lobby. The person who answered the phone was friendly. They signed the admissions agreement, twenty-five pages of single-spaced text, in twenty minutes, in a hallway, with their father waiting upstairs.

I have watched some version of this scene play out hundreds of times over the course of my career. The details change. The names change. Sometimes it's a stroke instead of a fall. Sometimes it's a spouse calling from a psychiatric hospital after a violent episode of dementia-related behavior. Sometimes it's an adult child who has been providing all of the care themselves, quietly, for three years, and has finally, completely, broken down. But the core of the story is almost always the same.

The family wasn't ready. And now they have no time.

Who This Book Is For

You may be reading this because something has already shifted. Maybe you've noticed that your mother seems more forgetful than she used to be. Maybe your father had a fall last month that scared you both. Maybe your spouse has been diagnosed with something — Parkinson's, Alzheimer's, advancing heart disease, and you're beginning to understand, quietly, that the trajectory has changed.

Or maybe you're more like Karen than you'd like to admit. You're already in it. You're already making the drives, the calls, the quiet arrangements nobody asked you to make. You're managing someone else's life alongside your own and doing it without a roadmap, hoping the next step will become clear before you need it.

Or you may be reading this simply because you're the kind of person who plans ahead. You've watched friends navigate this with their parents and you want to be ready. You've done the estate planning, you have the will, and now you're turning your attention to the question nobody talks about at the financial planner's office: what happens when someone I love can no longer live independently, and how do I make sure we handle it well?

Either way, this book is for you.

Specifically, it is written for:

Adult children who are beginning to worry about an aging parent, whether the concern is new or has been quietly growing for years

Spouses and partners watching a loved one change — caught between fierce loyalty, exhaustion, and the growing awareness that you cannot do this alone forever

Anyone who wants to make this decision thoughtfully, rather than frantically

This book is not a medical textbook. It is not a legal manual. It will not tell you exactly what Medicare covers in your state this year, because those rules change and you should always verify current information with the appropriate professionals. What it will give you is the roadmap — the questions to ask, the factors to weigh, the conversations to have, and the knowledge to walk into any facility, any financial meeting, any family discussion, with your eyes open and your footing sure.

What This Book Is Not

Before we go further, let me be clear about what you won't find here.

This is not a book that will make the decision for you. Every family is different. Every person's health, financial situation, family geography, and personal history is different. My job is to give you the tools, not to tell you which care setting is right for your loved one, because I don't know your situation, and anyone who claims they can make that call without knowing your situation is selling you something.

This is not a book that will make the emotional part easy. It won't. I have never met a family for whom placing a loved one in a care facility was simple, clean, or free of grief. What I can do, and what I hope this book does — is help you separate the emotional weight of the decision from the practical paralysis that comes from not knowing what you're doing. You can carry the emotion. What you don't have to carry is the confusion.

And this is not a book that treats placement as failure. If I believed that, I could not have spent 34 years in this field. The skilled nursing facilities, assisted living communities, and memory care units I have seen at their best are remarkable places — staffed by people who have chosen, every day, to show up for some of the most vulnerable members of our society. When a family has done the work of finding the right place and making the transition thoughtfully, the outcome is often better than what came before. More support. More safety. More engagement. More peace of mind, for the resident, and for the family.

The goal is not to avoid these places. The goal is to choose the right one, at the right time, for the right reasons.

The Four Scenarios I've Seen Too Many Times

In my years working in admissions, I watched families arrive in crisis in essentially four ways. Each one represents a version of waiting too long, and each one is avoidable with planning.

The Hospital Discharge Crisis

This is Karen's story. It is the most common scenario I encountered. A medical event, a fall, a stroke, a cardiac episode, a serious infection — results in a hospitalization. The hospital stabilizes the patient and then, because hospitals are acute care settings not designed for long-term convalescence, begins the process of discharge planning almost immediately.

The family, who may have been managing their loved one's care for months or years, suddenly faces a hard deadline. 48 hours. 72 hours. Maybe a week. Choose a facility. Sign the paperwork. Make one of the most consequential decisions of your family's life under conditions of maximum stress, minimum information, and zero preparation.

Families in this situation frequently choose based on the wrong things — proximity alone, a nice lobby, a friendly voice on the phone, because they have no basis for choosing based on the right things. They sign admissions agreements without understanding them. They miss questions they should have asked. And they carry the uncertainty of that rushed decision for months or years afterward.

The Fall or Event That Forces the Issue

Sometimes the crisis is not a hospitalization but a single event that can no longer be explained away. A fall that results in a call from a neighbor. A car accident. A fire on the stove. A missed medication that causes a medical emergency. An incident that makes it impossible, finally, undeniably, to maintain the story that everything is fine.

These events are often the moment when adult children realize they have been managing a slow-motion emergency for a long time without naming it as such. The fall didn't come from nowhere. The cognitive decline that contributed to it has been visible for months. But the family wasn't ready to act, and so they waited, and now the decision is being made in the aftermath of an event that could sometimes have been prevented.

The Condition That Deteriorated Beyond What Anyone Admitted

This is perhaps the most painful pattern to witness, and the most common in cases involving dementia. A person's condition declines gradually, and the family adjusts to each new baseline so slowly that they lose their frame of reference for what is normal. What would have been alarming a year ago has become the new ordinary. The person can no longer reliably recognize family members, but they still seem like themselves on good days. The incontinence has become constant, but the family has found a routine. The wandering is dangerous, but the house has been locked.

By the time many of these families arrive at an admissions office, the loved one's condition is significantly more advanced than could have been safely managed at home for some time. The transition is harder, the adjustment is harder, and the guilt, the terrible, misplaced guilt of feeling that waiting somehow represented love — is harder.

It did not represent love. It represented the very human difficulty of acknowledging a truth you are not ready to accept. This book is designed to help you accept it earlier, so the transition can happen on your terms rather than the disease's.

The Caregiver Who Broke

The fourth scenario is one that rarely gets discussed openly, which means it carries an extra layer of shame it does not deserve.

Family caregiving is one of the most demanding things a human being can do. It is physically exhausting, emotionally isolating, financially costly, and socially invisible. The spouses and adult children who provide primary care, often for years, often while simultaneously raising families, maintaining careers, and managing their own health — are doing something extraordinary. And they frequently do it past the point of sustainability, because asking for help feels like failure, and considering placement feels like abandonment, and there is no roadmap that tells them when it is acceptable to say: I cannot do this alone anymore.

I have sat with caregivers who had not slept more than three hours in a night for months. Who had stopped seeing friends, stopped exercising, stopped tending to medical conditions of their own. Who had given everything they had and more, and were still convinced they were failing.

They were not failing. They were drowning. And the right facility, at the right time, with the right level of care, would have been a lifeline, for the person receiving care, and for the person providing it.

> *If you are the caregiver in this story, please hear this: taking care of yourself is not separate from taking care of*

your loved one. It is the same act. You cannot provide good care from an empty reserve, and you are not required to destroy yourself to prove your love.

How This Book Is Organized

This book moves through the decision in the order families actually need to think about it. We begin with the territory — what these care settings actually are, and how they differ from one another, because confusion about the basic terminology causes real harm at the point of decision. We move through the question of timing, then the health and medical factors that drive placement decisions, and then the financial reality that shapes what is possible for most families.

We spend considerable time on quality — how to evaluate a facility before you trust it with someone you love, and on the practical and logistical factors that shape the decision: location, the family dynamics that complicate every major decision, and the legal documents that must be in place before a crisis makes them impossible to obtain.

Each chapter ends with a Key Takeaways section and a single Action Step, one concrete thing you can do before moving to the next chapter. By the time you reach the end of this book, you will have completed what I call The When Readiness Checklist: a comprehensive planning tool built piece by piece across each chapter, designed so that when the moment of decision arrives, most of the hard work will already be done.

I have also included, where relevant, notes from my own experience — things I observed in admissions that families almost never knew to ask about, patterns I saw in facilities that separated good care from the appearance of it, and moments from 34 years in this field that I believe belong in this book because they are true and because they might help you.

One More Thing Before We Begin

If you have picked up this book because someone you love is already in crisis, if the call has already come and you are already in the waiting room — I want you to know that this book will still help you. Turn to Chapter Six on quality evaluation and Chapter Eight on making the decision. You will find what you need.

But if you are reading this before the crisis arrives, if you are in that window of time when there are still choices to be made, when the decision is not yet upon you — then you are holding something valuable. You are holding the opportunity to do this differently than most families do. To approach one of the hardest decisions you will ever face with information, preparation, and the quiet confidence that comes from knowing what you're doing.

That is what this book is for.

Let's begin.

Key Takeaways from the Introduction

The families who suffer most in the long-term care placement process are those who had no plan, not because they didn't care, but because no one told them they needed one.

There are four common patterns of waiting too long: hospital discharge crisis, a sudden fall or event, a condition that deteriorated past what anyone admitted, and caregiver burnout.

This book is not about giving up. It is about giving your loved one the best possible care, in the right place, at the right time, without the chaos that comes from deciding in crisis.

Placement is not failure. When chosen thoughtfully and at the right time, the right care setting often produces better outcomes — more support, more safety, more engagement — than what was possible at home.

If you are the primary caregiver: taking care of yourself is not separate from taking care of your loved one. You cannot pour from an empty reserve.

ACTION STEP:

Before reading Chapter One, have an honest 10-minute conversation with yourself, or with a spouse or sibling if appropriate. Ask: if something happened tomorrow, would we know what to do? Would we know what our loved one's wishes are? Would we know how the finances work? Write down the three things you are most uncertain about. Those are the questions this book is going to answer.

Before a family can make a good decision about where a loved one should go, they need to understand the picture — what these places actually are, how they differ, and what each one is designed to do. Chapter One, The World of Long-Term Care: Know Before You Go, gives you the map.

CHAPTER ONE

The World of Long-Term Care: Know Before You Go

A CONVERSATION I'VE HAD MORE TIMES THAN I CAN COUNT

Margaret had done her homework. That was the thing — she wasn't someone who made decisions carelessly. A year before anything happened, she'd spent several weeks looking into assisted living options near her mother's home in suburban Cleveland: touring communities, comparing amenities and pricing, talking to a friend who'd recently gone through the same thing with her own father. She'd identified a community she felt good about — warm staff, good location, a memory care wing if it ever came to that. She had a folder. She had notes.

She thought she was ready.

Then her mother fell. A bad fall — hospitalization, surgery, the works. And suddenly Margaret was in a conference room with a hospital social worker who was kind, clearly overworked, and needed a discharge decision within 72 hours.

The community Margaret had researched a year earlier was unable to handle her mother's skilled needs. A second facility on her list had changed ownership and the reviews had turned. The social worker handed her a new list on a piece of paper — facilities that possibly had current openings, and most of them were names Margaret had never looked at. The folder she'd prepared, the notes she'd taken, the decision she thought she'd already made: none of it transferred.

She was starting over. Under deadline. With her mother waiting upstairs.

What Margaret didn't have — what would have actually helped her in that moment — wasn't more research. It was a foundation. An understanding of what these different settings actually are, what questions to ask of any facility regardless of its name or rating, and what her mother's specific needs meant for the type of care she required. That knowledge would have traveled with her. The folder didn't.

I have had some version of this conversation more times than I can count. Families who prepared, who really tried, and still found themselves lost when the moment arrived, because the preparation was pointed at the wrong things. This chapter is an attempt to give you the right things. Before we talk about timing, finances, or how to evaluate quality, you need to understand what these places actually are — what they do, what they don't do, and what the differences mean for the person you're trying to care for.

The Spectrum of Care: Four Settings, Four Different Purposes

Long-term care is not one thing. It is a spectrum, a range of settings designed to meet different levels of need, from the relatively independent older adult who simply wants community and convenience, to the medically complex patient who requires round-the-clock skilled nursing. Understanding where your loved one falls on that spectrum, and how that may change over time — is the foundation of every good placement decision.

There are four primary care settings you need to understand. Each one is distinct in terms of what care it provides, how it is regulated, and how it is paid for. Knowing the difference before a crisis arrives is exactly the kind of foundation that Margaret didn't have, and that this chapter is designed to give you.

Independent Living: A Lifestyle Choice, Not a Care Setting

Independent living communities, sometimes called retirement communities, senior apartments, or active adult communities — are designed for older adults who are largely self-sufficient and want the convenience, community, and amenities of a shared setting without the responsibilities of maintaining a home.

These communities typically offer dining options, transportation, social programming, fitness facilities, and housekeeping. Residents may still drive, maintain active social lives, and manage their own schedules and medical care. What the community itself does not provide is care. There are no nurses on staff, no medication management, no help with bathing or dressing. If a resident's health declines to the point where they need those services, they will need to either arrange them independently — through home health aides, for example, or transition to a higher level of care.

Independent living is paid for privately. It is not covered by Medicare or, in most cases, Medicaid. The monthly cost varies enormously by location and amenity level, but families should understand this clearly: it is a real estate and lifestyle decision, not a care placement.

> *Independent living can be a wonderful choice for the right person at the right time. The mistake is choosing it when someone actually needs care, or failing to plan for the transition when the need for care eventually arrives.*

Assisted Living: Support for Daily Life — With Important Limits

Assisted living is where many families begin their search, and for good reason: it is the setting that closely resembles home while still providing meaningful support. Assisted living communities are designed for adults who need help with some activities of daily living — bathing, dressing, grooming, meal preparation, medication management, but who do not require the level of medical care provided in a skilled nursing facility.

A good assisted living community offers private or semi-private apartments, communal dining, social activities, and staff available around the clock to assist with personal care. Many feel more like residential communities than medical facilities, which is intentional and, for the right resident, appropriate.

Here is what assisted living is not: it is not a medical setting. Assisted living staff can help with medications, but they are not licensed to administer skilled nursing care. They can assist with personal hygiene, but they are not equipped to manage complex wounds, IV therapy, or medically complex conditions. Many assisted living communities do not have a nurse on-site 24 hours a day, or if they do, the staffing levels are not comparable to a skilled nursing facility.

This distinction matters enormously when a person's needs increase. Assisted living communities have the right, and in many cases the obligation — to ask a resident to leave if their care needs exceed what the community is licensed and staffed to provide. That said, some communities will allow a resident to remain in place by bringing in private duty home care to supplement what the community offers — though this comes at additional cost and varies by facility and state regulation. Families who understand this option early have more flexibility than those who discover it under pressure.

Families who don't understand these limits can find themselves scrambling to find a new placement at exactly the moment they can least afford to be scrambling.

> **COMMON MYTH:** *"The assisted living will handle her medications and any medical issues that come up."*
>
> **THE REALITY:** Assisted living can help manage medications — organizing them, reminding residents to take them, and in some states, administering them, but this is not skilled medical care. Complex medical needs, wounds, IVs, and clinical monitoring require a licensed skilled nursing facility.

Memory Care: Specialized Support — But Not Standardized

Memory care refers to a specialized level of care for adults with Alzheimer's disease, other forms of dementia, or cognitive impairments that affect their safety and daily functioning. Memory care units are typically secured — meaning residents cannot exit without assistance, and staffed by people trained specifically in dementia care.

What memory care is not, at the federal level, is a defined regulatory category. In most states, memory care is a designation, a wing, a floor, a specialized program — within either an assisted living community or a skilled nursing facility. The problem is that there is no federal standard for what 'memory care' actually requires. Any facility can market itself as a memory care provider. The training requirements, staffing ratios, and programming that distinguish excellent memory care from a locked wing with a sign are matters of state regulation and individual facility quality, which vary enormously.

This is one of the areas where doing your homework matters most, and where the guidance in Chapter Six on evaluating quality will be particularly important. Because the term is not federally standardized, the difference between excellent memory care and a secured unit with limited specialized programming comes down to questions most families don't know to ask. When evaluating any memory care program, those questions — about staffing, training, and how behavioral symptoms are managed — are not optional courtesies. They are the difference between a setting where your loved one will be well supported and one where they will simply be safe from wandering.

COMMON MYTH: *"Any facility that says it has memory care is equipped to handle my mother's Alzheimer's."*

THE REALITY: Memory care is not a federally standardized category. The term describes a level of programming and environment, but what that actually looks like varies significantly from facility to facility, and the gap between excellent memory care and the minimum can be wide. Before placing a loved one in any memory care program, ask specific questions about staff training, ratios, programming, and how behavioral symptoms are managed. We cover exactly what to ask in Chapter Six.

Skilled Nursing Facilities: The Most Regulated, and Most Misunderstood — Setting

Skilled nursing facilities — still called nursing homes in common parlance, and SNFs in industry shorthand — are the most clinically intensive of the four settings. They provide 24-hour nursing care, access to licensed therapists (physical, occupational, and speech), and the capacity to manage medically complex conditions: wound care, IV therapy, feeding tubes, ventilator support, complex medication regimens, and post-surgical recovery, among others.

SNFs are the most heavily regulated care setting in long-term care, subject to both federal and state oversight and required to undergo regular inspections. They are also the setting most families have the most fear about, a fear that is sometimes warranted and sometimes based on outdated assumptions or the experience of a bad facility that should not be generalized to all of them.

One of the most important distinctions in understanding skilled nursing facilities is the difference between short-term rehabilitation and long-term care. Both happen in the same building, sometimes on the same floor, and from the outside they can be indistinguishable. But they are fundamentally different situations, governed by different payment structures and carrying very different prognoses.

One thing worth noting here, and we will return to this in later chapters — is that couples facing different levels of care need not necessarily be separated. Many skilled nursing facilities and continuing care campuses can accommodate spouses who need different levels of care on the same property, even if not in the same room or unit. It is worth asking this question early, because the answer directly shapes which facilities belong on your list.

> **COMMON MYTH:** *"She's going to the nursing home for rehab — so Medicare will cover it."*

> **THE REALITY:** Medicare does cover short-term skilled nursing care under specific conditions: a qualifying hospital stay of at least three days, admission within 30 days of discharge, and a documented need for skilled services. Traditional Medicare generally requires this three-day inpatient hospital stay, although some Medicare Advantage plans waive this requirement. But there are two things families often don't realize: Medicare coverage is time-limited — 100 days maximum per benefit period, with steep co-pays after day 20, and those 100 days are not guaranteed. Medicare requires ongoing documentation that the patient is making measurable progress. If progress stalls, coverage can end well before day 100. We cover this in detail in the next section.

> **COMMON MYTH:** *"Medicare will pay for the nursing home if she runs out of money."*

> **THE REALITY:** This is one of the most persistent and costly misconceptions in long-term care planning. Medicare does not pay for long-term custodial care in a skilled nursing facility. Medicaid does, but only after a person has spent down their assets to qualify, and only in facilities that accept Medicaid. The rules are complex, state-specific, and require advance planning to navigate well. Chapter Five covers the financial picture in full.

Short-Term Rehab vs. Long-Term Care: The Distinction That Confuses Everyone

Because this confusion is so common and so consequential, it deserves its own section.

When an older adult has a hospitalization, a hip fracture, a stroke, a serious illness — they are often discharged to a skilled nursing facility for rehabilitation. Physical therapists work to help them regain mobility. Occupational therapists help them relearn daily tasks. Speech therapists help residents regain the ability to speak and overcome challenges with swallowing. The goal is recovery and return to a less intensive setting, ideally home.

This is short-term skilled nursing care, and it looks very different from long-term placement. Residents in short-term rehab are typically there for days or weeks. They are engaged in active therapy. The expectation — shared by the resident, the family, and the facility — is discharge.

Long-term care is something different. A person in long-term skilled nursing care has needs that are not expected to resolve with rehabilitation — chronic medical conditions requiring ongoing nursing supervision, advanced dementia, or a level of physical dependence that cannot safely be managed at home or in a lower level of care. Long-term care residents may live in a skilled nursing facility for months or years.

The reason this distinction matters so much is threefold. First, the payment structures are completely different: Medicare covers short-term skilled care under specific conditions; it does not cover long-term custodial care. Second, the emotional and practical experience for the resident and family is entirely different, one is a temporary setback, the other is a permanent transition. Third, the evaluation criteria you should use when choosing a facility are different depending on which situation you're in.

> *If your loved one is in a skilled nursing facility for rehabilitation after a hospitalization, you may have more time than you think to plan their next step. Use it. The chapters on timing, quality, and financial planning ahead will help you do exactly that.*

The Continuum, and Why Needs Change

One of the most important things to understand about long-term care is that it is not a single decision. It is often a series of decisions over time, as a person's needs evolve.

Someone may begin in independent living and transition to assisted living when daily support becomes necessary. They may move from assisted living to a memory care program as dementia progresses, and from memory care to skilled nursing when their medical needs exceed what a residential setting can provide. Some people move through several of these settings. Others land in one place and stay. Some go from home directly to skilled nursing without ever passing through the intermediate settings.

There is no single right path, but there is a right level of care for each stage of a person's needs. Understanding the territory means understanding not just where your loved one is today, but where they may be heading, and what the next step might look like before they need it.

For families who want to plan ahead and minimize the number of disruptive transitions their loved one will face, there is one option worth understanding in more depth: the continuing care retirement community, or CCRC.

A CCRC is not simply a retirement community — it is a campus that offers multiple levels of care in a single location: typically independent living, assisted living, memory care, and skilled nursing. A resident can move through those levels as their needs change without leaving their community, their social connections, or their sense of place. For couples where one partner eventually needs a higher level of care than the other, a CCRC campus can mean the difference between living apart and remaining close.

The options within CCRCs vary considerably. Some offer villa-style living — townhome or cottage arrangements that feel more like private residences than institutional settings. Others offer apartment-style living with varying levels of amenity and community programming. The common thread is the continuum: the ability to age in place on a single campus rather than moving between unrelated facilities as needs evolve.

CCRCs typically require a major financial commitment — entrance fees that can range from modest to substantial, plus monthly fees, and they come with their own contractual structures that deserve careful review. We will address the financial considerations in Chapter Five. For now, the point is this: for the right family at the right time, a CCRC can be one of the most thoughtful long-term care decisions available. The key is making it proactively — while your loved one is still well enough to be accepted and to enjoy what the community offers, rather than arriving at the option only when crisis forces the question.

At a Glance: The Four Settings Compared

The table below summarizes the key distinctions across the four care settings. Keep it as a reference as you read the chapters ahead.

Care Setting	Who It's For	Medical Care Provided?	Typically Paid By	The Key Distinction
Independent Living	Healthy older adults who want community, amenities, and less home maintenance	None — this is housing, not care	Private pay only	*Lifestyle choice, not care placement. No licensing for medical services.*
Assisted Living	Adults needing help with daily activities: bathing, dressing, medications, meals	Limited. Help with medications and ADLs, not skilled nursing or medical treatment	Primarily private pay. Some long-term care insurance. Medicaid in some states (limited).	*NOT a substitute for skilled nursing. Regulations vary widely by state.*
Memory Care	Adults with Alzheimer's, dementia, or other cognitive impairments requiring a secure environment	Dementia-specialized support and supervision, not skilled medical care	Primarily private pay. Long-term care insurance. Some Medicaid waiver programs.	*Often a wing within an AL facility. No federal standard for what 'memory care' requires.*
Skilled Nursing Facility (SNF)	Adults needing 24-hour nursing care, post-acute rehabilitation, or complex medical management	Yes. Licensed nurses and therapists on-site 24/7. Wound care, IV therapy, PT/OT, and more.	Medicare (short-term rehab, with conditions). Medicaid (long-term, income-based). Managed Care plans. Private pay.	*Most regulated setting. Short-term rehab is very different from long-term placement — same building, different purpose.*

A note on terminology: throughout this book, I will use 'skilled nursing facility' and 'SNF' to refer to licensed nursing homes providing 24-hour skilled care. I will use 'nursing home' only when quoting families, because that is the language most people use, even though it has become a somewhat imprecise term that can refer to several different settings. When precision matters, I will be precise.

Key Takeaways from Chapter One

Long-term care is a spectrum of four distinct settings — independent living, assisted living, memory care, and skilled nursing — each designed for different levels of need and governed by different regulations and payment structures.

Independent living is a lifestyle and housing choice, not a care placement. It provides no medical or personal care services.

Assisted living supports daily living activities but is not equipped for complex medical care. Care needs that exceed what a community is licensed to provide will result in a required transfer.

Memory care is not federally standardized. Any facility can use the term. The quality of memory care programming varies enormously, and requires specific questions to evaluate.

Skilled nursing facilities are the most clinically intensive setting and the most regulated. Short-term rehabilitation and long-term care happen in the same buildings but are fundamentally different situations with different payment rules.

Medicare does not cover long-term custodial care. Medicaid does, but only under specific financial eligibility rules that require advance planning to navigate.

Long-term care is rarely a single decision. Needs change over time, and understanding the full continuum helps families anticipate the next transition before they are forced into it.

ACTION STEP:

> *Using the comparison table, identify which care setting best matches your loved one's current needs, and which setting might be the next step if their condition progresses. If you're not sure, that uncertainty is useful information: it tells you where the gaps in your planning are. Write down your answers and bring them to the When Readiness Checklist at the end of the book.*

Now that you have the map, we turn to the hardest question in this book: when. Chapter Two, The Question of When, is the emotional heart of this guide, the chapter that takes head-on the question families avoid, delay, and agonize over. We'll look at the signals that matter, the ones that don't, and how to tell the difference between appropriate caution and denial that has gone on too long.

CHAPTER TWO

The Question of When

TWENTY-THREE HOURS

For a long time, the family told themselves it wasn't that bad.

It had started small, the way it always does. Eleanor — sharp, funny, the kind of woman who had opinions about everything and was usually right — began to repeat herself. A story told at dinner that had been told at lunch. A name that slipped away mid-sentence and didn't come back. Her husband Frank noticed first, and did what a lot of spouses do: he covered for her. Gently redirected conversations. Answered questions that had been directed at Eleanor before the pause became awkward. He told himself it was normal aging. He told himself she was fine.

Their three children — David, Susan, and the youngest, Patrice — noticed too. They talked about it among themselves, in the careful, lowered tones that families use when they're discussing something nobody wants to say out loud. They agreed it was something to keep an eye on. They did not agree on what to do about it, and so they did nothing. Nobody wanted to be the one to say the word. Nobody wanted to upset Frank. Nobody wanted to look at Eleanor across the dinner table and see, in her eyes, that she knew what they were thinking.

The years passed. Eleanor's world got smaller. She stopped driving — Frank had quietly taken the keys after she came home one afternoon unable to explain where she'd been. She stopped cooking, then stopped wanting to go out, then stopped recognizing the neighbors she'd known for thirty years. Frank managed it all. He took over the grocery shopping, the medications, the bills. He stopped sleeping through the night. He lost weight. When the children visited, he smiled and said things were fine. They wanted to believe him.

No one talked about what came next. Not because they didn't love Eleanor or Frank. Because talking about it felt like giving up on them.

Then came the night Eleanor walked out the back door at 2 a.m.

Frank woke to an empty bed and found the door ajar. He called her name through the house, then through the yard, then called David, who called Susan, who called Patrice, who called the police. For twenty-three hours, Eleanor was missing. She was found the following evening, two miles from home, dehydrated and frightened.

She was taken to the hospital. Frank sat in the waiting room with his three children for the first time in years, and nobody talked in lowered tones anymore.

David was relieved — so overwhelmingly, almost guiltily relieved that she was safe that he couldn't feel anything else yet.

Susan was already grieving, quietly and completely, for the mother she'd been losing in pieces for years. Patrice was angry, not at anyone in particular, but at the years of circling, the conversations that never happened, the decisions that had been deferred until deferral was no longer an option.

And Frank — Frank was all three. Relief and grief and anger, and underneath all of it, the thing he had never been able to say: he was exhausted. He had been exhausted for years. And even now, sitting in a hospital waiting room at midnight, he was not sure he could bring himself to do what everyone in that room knew had to happen next. Because doing it felt, to him, like giving up on his wife. Like failing the promise he had made her.

It was not giving up. It was not failure. But no one had ever told him that, and he had never asked.

This chapter is about the question that families never asked until a crisis forces it. It is about how to ask it earlier, and how to recognize, before the night of the open door, that the time to ask it has arrived.

The Hard Truth About Timing

There is no perfect moment to make a care placement decision. Families who wait for one, for the moment when everyone agrees, when the guilt lifts, when the right answer becomes obvious, often find that the decision is eventually made for them, under conditions they would never have chosen.

What I have observed over 34 years is this: earlier is almost always better. Not because earlier is easier — it isn't. The grief is the same. The guilt is the same. But earlier means choices. It means time to research, to visit facilities, to have the conversations that need to happen before a crisis makes them impossible. It means your loved one may be well enough to participate in the decision. It means the transition can happen on your terms rather than a hospital discharge planner's deadline.

The families I have watched get through this well are not the ones who felt no guilt. They felt exactly the same guilt as everyone else. What separated them was that they found a way to act in spite of it, because they understood, or came to understand, that waiting was not a neutral choice. Every week of delay had a cost. Sometimes that cost was measured in safety. Sometimes in caregiver health. Sometimes, as with Frank and Eleanor, in a night that could have ended very differently.

> *Waiting is not the same as loving. And acting is not the same as giving up. The decision to find the right care at the right time is one of the most loving things a family can do, for the person who needs care, and for the people providing it.*

So how do you know when earlier is now? The signals are rarely sudden. They accumulate, the way Frank's exhaustion accumulated, the way Eleanor's world got smaller one thing at a time. This chapter will help you see them, and take them seriously before the night of the open door.

Why Families Wait — And Why It Makes Sense

Before we get to the signals, it is worth naming the forces that work against acting on them. Because the delay is not irrational. It is deeply human, and understanding it is the first step toward moving through it.

The most common reason families wait is the one Frank lived: the belief that placement equals abandonment. That a good spouse, a good child, a good family takes care of their own — at home, by themselves, for as long as possible. This belief is almost never stated out loud, but it operates powerfully beneath every conversation that doesn't happen, every signal that gets explained away, every year that passes while a caregiver quietly disappears into their role.

The second reason is denial, and denial, at its root, is usually love. Acknowledging that a parent or spouse needs a level of care you cannot provide means acknowledging the progression of something you would give anything to stop. Families don't look away because they don't care. They look away because looking directly is almost unbearable.

The third reason is the family dynamic itself. Placement decisions rarely involve just one person. They involve siblings who live in different cities and have different relationships with the person who needs care. A spouse whose grief takes a different form than their children's. Old family patterns that resurface under pressure. Someone who wants to act and someone who isn't ready, and the paralysis that settles in between them. We will address family dynamics in depth in Chapter Seven. For now, the point is simply this: the difficulty of these conversations is real, and it is one of the reasons the signals get ignored longer than they should.

> *You are not wrong for finding this hard. You are not wrong for wanting more time. What this chapter asks of you is not that you stop feeling those things — it is that you learn to act alongside them.*

The Signals: What to Look For and What It Means

The signals that a person needs a higher level of care than they are currently receiving fall into four categories. They rarely appear in isolation. More often, they accumulate across categories, a safety concern here, a medical pattern there, a caregiver who is visibly struggling — until the weight of them becomes undeniable. Learning to read them is not about finding a single threshold to cross. It is about developing the habit of honest observation.

Safety Signals

Safety is often the category that families notice first, and explain away longest. A fall becomes "she's always been clumsy." A burner on the stove left on becomes "everyone forgets sometimes." A fender bender becomes "traffic is terrible." The explanations aren't dishonest — they're a natural response to observations we aren't ready to act on. But the pattern they form, over time, tells a story.

The safety signals that warrant serious attention include:

Falls, especially recurring incidents, falls without a clear cause, or falls that result in injury. A single fall can be an isolated event. Multiple falls in a six-month period are a pattern, and a pattern is a predictor.

Wandering or getting lost — leaving the home unsafely, becoming disoriented in familiar places, being unable to find the way home. This is one of the most serious safety signals in dementia and one of the clearest indicators that the current living situation is no longer adequate.

Medication errors — missed doses, double doses, confusion about what medications are for. Medication mismanagement is one of the leading causes of preventable hospitalization in older adults.

Driving concerns — getting lost on familiar routes, unexplained damage to the vehicle, near-misses reported by others, or a pattern of minor accidents. The conversation about driving is one of the hardest families have, and one of the most necessary.

Home safety — evidence of falls that weren't reported, burn marks on counters or cookware, spoiled food not noticed or discarded, unlocked doors at night, or a home environment that has deteriorated in ways the person seems unaware of.

The guilt that accompanies these observations is usually proportional to their severity, which is to say, the more alarming the signal, the harder it often is to name it directly. What helps is separating observation from decision. Noticing that your father has fallen three times in two months is not the same as deciding his future. It is simply paying attention to what is true.

Medical and Clinical Signals

Some of the most important signals are the ones that require a medical lens to fully understand, which is why having an honest relationship with your loved one's physician is one of the most valuable things a family can cultivate before a crisis. Doctors often see the trajectory more clearly than families do, precisely because they are not in the middle of it emotionally.

The medical and clinical signals to pay attention to include:

Diagnosis trajectory — certain diagnoses carry predictable progressions. Alzheimer's and other dementias, Parkinson's disease, congestive heart failure, COPD, and ALS all follow patterns that, while variable in their timing, are not variable in their direction. Understanding the trajectory of a diagnosis means you can plan for what is coming rather than reacting to it.

Increasing hospitalizations, a pattern of hospitalizations, especially for the same or related conditions, often signals that the current level of care is no longer sufficient to manage a person's medical needs safely at home.

Weight loss and nutritional decline — unexplained weight loss, skipped meals, a refrigerator full of untouched food, or difficulty swallowing are signals that should be taken seriously. Nutritional decline accelerates cognitive and physical deterioration.

Decline in personal hygiene, a person who has always been meticulous about their appearance showing up in unwashed clothes, going days without bathing, or being unable to manage basic grooming tasks is signaling something important about their functional capacity.

Unmanaged chronic conditions — blood pressure consistently out of range, blood sugar poorly controlled, wounds not healing, infections recurring. When chronic conditions that were previously managed begin to spiral, it often means the management system, which may be relying heavily on a caregiver — is no longer adequate.

A word about physicians: many families assume that the doctor will tell them when it is time. Sometimes that happens. More often, the physician sees the patient for fifteen minutes every few months and is working with incomplete information about what daily life actually looks like. The family is the expert on daily life. If you are observing things that concern you, say so directly — "I am worried about his safety at home and I want to know what you are seeing", rather than waiting for the physician to raise it first.

Do not be afraid to advocate. Do not be afraid to ask questions, or to say that you don't understand something and need it explained differently. You are not bothering anyone. You are doing your job as the person who knows this patient best outside of a clinical setting. The families who get the most useful information from medical appointments are the ones who come prepared to ask, not just to listen.

A note: I am not a medical professional, and nothing in this book should be taken as medical advice. The signals described here are patterns I have observed over decades of working with families, not clinical diagnoses. Your loved one's own physicians and care team are always the right source for specific medical guidance.

Social and Emotional Signals

These are the signals that are easiest to dismiss and, in some ways, the most telling. A person who has withdrawn from the activities and relationships that defined their life is telling you something, not always in words, and not always consciously, but clearly, if you are paying attention.

The social and emotional signals that warrant attention include:

Withdrawal from social life — stopping activities they previously loved, declining invitations, losing interest in relationships. Isolation both accelerates cognitive decline and masks it, making it harder for families to get an accurate picture of how their loved one is doing.

Depression and anxiety — persistent sadness, tearfulness, expressions of hopelessness or worthlessness, or marked increase in anxiety. Depression is common among older adults and consistently undertreated. It is also a signal, in combination with other indicators, that the current situation is not sustainable.

Self-neglect, not just hygiene, but the broader pattern of a person who has stopped taking care of themselves in ways that go beyond what aging alone explains. Unpaid bills, a home in disrepair, postponed medical appointments, prescription refills not picked up.

Personality or behavioral changes — increased irritability, suspicion, emotional volatility, or behavior that is notably out of character. In dementia particularly, behavioral changes are often the signal that families find hardest to name because they can feel like a betrayal of the person they know to describe them. Wandering, listed under safety signals, is also rooted here: it is as much an expression of disorientation and emotional distress as it is a physical risk.

Expressions of fear or confusion, a person who says they are scared, who seems frequently disoriented, who expresses uncertainty about where they are or what is happening, is communicating a need that deserves a direct response.

The guilt that accompanies these observations often takes a particular form: the worry that noticing these things, and acting on them, means you are giving up on the person your parent or spouse used to be. It doesn't. It means you are taking the person they are now seriously enough to get them the help they actually need.

Caregiver Signals

This category is the one most likely to be missing from other books on this subject, because the focus is usually on the person receiving care. But the condition of the caregiver is one of the most reliable signals that a placement decision can no longer be deferred, and it is a signal that the caregiver themselves is almost always the last to name.

Frank's story is the template. He was managing Eleanor's care for years while his own health deteriorated, his sleep disappeared, and his world narrowed to the dimensions of their house. His children could see it. He could not, or could not afford to. Naming his own exhaustion felt, to him, like a complaint. Like weakness. Like not loving her enough.

It was none of those things. It was data. And it was telling him, clearly, that the current situation was not sustainable — for Eleanor, or for him.

The caregiver signals that warrant serious attention include:

Physical exhaustion — chronic sleep deprivation, weight loss, declining personal health, medical appointments of their own being skipped or postponed. A caregiver who is physically depleted cannot provide good care, and will not be able to for long.

Emotional depletion — persistent sadness, anxiety, emotional numbness, or the sense of going through the motions without being present. Caregiver burnout is a clinical reality with serious health consequences, not a character failing.

Social isolation, the caregiver's own world shrinking. No longer seeing friends, skipping family events, losing touch with the activities and relationships that sustained them. Isolation compounds every other form of caregiver stress.

Loss of safety — moments when the caregiver realizes they could not physically manage a fall, a behavioral episode, or a medical emergency on their own. This is one of the clearest signals that a solo caregiving arrangement has exceeded its capacity.

Resentment, not because the caregiver is a bad person, but because resentment is what happens when we give more than we have for longer than we can sustain. A caregiver who feels resentment and guilt about feeling resentment is a caregiver who is past the point of sustainability.

If you are the caregiver reading this and you recognize yourself in any of those signals: your condition is not a separate issue from your loved one's care. It is the same issue. The question of when is a question about both of you.

The Pattern Problem: Why We Stop Seeing What's in Front of Us

One of the most important things I observed in admissions, and one of the hardest to convey — is how completely families can lose their frame of reference for what is normal.

It happens gradually. A person's condition declines by small degrees, and the family adjusts to each new baseline so incrementally that they lose track of how far things have moved. The version of their loved one they are comparing to is not the person six months ago. It is the person from last week. And last week's baseline has already incorporated a dozen small declines they no longer register as declines.

I have sat with families in admissions offices who described their loved one's condition in terms that were notably at odds with what I was observing in the room. Not because they were dishonest. Because they had been inside the situation so long that they could no longer see it from the outside.

There are a few tools that can help restore perspective:

Talk to someone who hasn't seen your loved one recently, a relative who visits infrequently, an old friend. Their reaction to the current situation is often a more accurate gauge than yours, precisely because they haven't adjusted to each incremental change.

Keep a simple log, not an elaborate system, just a note when something concerning happens. A fall. A medication error. An episode of confusion. Looking back at three months of notes is a different experience than trying to remember how things have been.

Ask the physician directly — 'compared to where she was a year ago, how would you describe her trajectory?' Frame it as a request for honest information, not reassurance.

Use the When Readiness Checklist at the end of this book — built specifically to give you an outside check when your own judgment has been compromised by proximity.

The goal is not to manufacture alarm. It is to see clearly, which is harder than it sounds when you love someone and you are in the middle of their story.

When You See the Signals: What Comes Next

Recognizing the signals is not the same as making the decision. And making the decision does not always mean immediate placement. There are bridge options — in-home care, adult day programs, respite stays, that can provide meaningful support while the larger decision takes shape. Chapter Three covers those options in full. For now, the point is simply this: seeing the signals clearly is the necessary first step, the one that transforms a vague, uncomfortable awareness into something you can actually work with.

When the signals are present, when you can see them clearly across one or more of the four categories, the next step is not to panic and not to act immediately. It is to start the process. Which means:

Having the honest conversations that have been deferred, with your siblings, your spouse, your loved one if they are able to participate. Chapter Seven covers how to handle these conversations in families where they are complicated.

Understanding what level of care the signals point to, which is exactly what Chapter One equipped you to assess.

Beginning to research your options before a deadline forces you to choose from whatever is available. The chapters on quality evaluation, financial planning, and location will equip you to do this well.

Making sure the legal documents are in place — power of attorney, healthcare proxy, advance directive. Chapter Ten covers this. If these documents don't exist yet, getting them in place is urgent regardless of where you are in the placement process.

What you do not need to do is have everything figured out before you start. The families who get through this best are not the ones who had a perfect plan. They are the ones who started early enough that imperfection was survivable, who gave themselves the gift of time that Frank and Eleanor's family never had.

What Happened to Frank

In the waiting room that night, with his three children around him and his wife being evaluated down the hall, Frank did something he had not been able to do in years. He talked.

Not about logistics. Not about what happened next. He talked about Eleanor — about who she was before, about the specific way she laughed, about the version of their life together he had been mourning, quietly, for longer than he had admitted to anyone including himself. And then he said, in a voice that his children would each remember differently for the rest of their lives: I don't know how to stop taking care of her myself. I don't know what that makes me.

The placement that followed was not without grief. It was not without difficulty. But it was the right decision, made at a moment when the family finally had no choice but to make it, and in a way, that absence of choice was a relief. The question they had been carrying for years had finally been answered, not by the night of the open door, but by what the family chose to do in its aftermath.

My hope, in writing this book, is that you don't need a night like that one to get there. That the signals in this chapter give you what Frank and Eleanor's family never had: the chance to answer the question before a crisis answers it for you.

Key Takeaways from Chapter Two

Earlier is almost always better. The families who navigate care placement well are not the ones who felt no guilt — they are the ones who found a way to act in spite of it, before a crisis removed their choices.

Waiting is not a neutral decision. Every week of delay has a cost — in safety, in caregiver health, in the quality of the transition when it eventually happens.

The signals accumulate across four categories: safety, medical and clinical, social and emotional, and caregiver condition. No single signal is a verdict. A pattern across categories is a clear message.

Families lose their frame of reference over time. The incremental nature of decline makes it easy to normalize what should not be normalized. Outside perspective, from infrequent visitors, physicians, or a structured tool like the When Readiness Checklist — can restore clarity.

The guilt and denial that surround this decision are not obstacles to overcome before you can act. They are feelings to carry alongside action. Waiting until they resolve is waiting forever.

The decision to find the right care at the right time is not giving up. It is one of the most loving things a family can do.

ACTION STEP:

Go through the four signal categories in this chapter — safety, medical and clinical, social and emotional, and caregiver condition, and write down, honestly, what you are observing in each one. Not what you hope is true, or what you can explain away, but what you actually see. If the signals are there, name them. That list is the beginning of the When Readiness Checklist, and it is the most important thing you will do before moving to Chapter Three.

Recognizing the signals is an important first step, but placement is not always the immediate next step. Chapter Three, Before the Move: Home Care, Respite, and the Options in Between, covers the bridge options that families often don't know exist: in-home care, adult day programs, and respite stays that can ease the transition, extend the timeline when appropriate, and give both caregivers and families room to breathe while the larger decision takes shape.

CHAPTER THREE

Before the Move: Home Care, Respite, and the Options in Between

THE CALL SHE WAS GLAD SHE MADE

Carol had been watching her mother for months. The signals were there, the ones from Chapter Two. Her mother, Ruth, was 74, living alone since Carol's father had passed two years earlier. She was still sharp in conversation, still knew everyone, still insisted she was fine. But the fine had started to fray at the edges. She was skipping meals. She'd stopped going to her garden club. The house, which Ruth had kept immaculately for fifty years, had started to slip.

Carol lived forty minutes away, close enough to visit but not close enough to be there every day. She was also still working, still raising a teenager at home, and increasingly aware that the mental bandwidth she was devoting to worrying about her mother was beginning to exceed what she could manage from a distance. She wasn't ready to talk about assisted living — her mother wasn't ready. But she knew something needed to change.

A friend suggested she call a geriatric care manager. Carol had never heard the term. She made the call mostly because she didn't know what else to do.

What happened over the next six months was not a dramatic rescue. It was something quieter and, in its own way, more valuable. The care manager assessed Ruth's situation and recommended a home care aide three mornings a week — help with meals, light housekeeping, medication reminders, and most importantly, company. She also connected Carol with an adult day program two afternoons a week that Ruth, to everyone's surprise, came to genuinely look forward to.

Ruth's decline did not stop. But it slowed, or at least became more manageable. When she did eventually transition to an assisted living community eighteen months later, she went in better health, with a clearer medical picture, and with Carol having had the time to research options carefully rather than in crisis. The transition was still hard. But it was a different kind of hard than it would have been without those eighteen months.

Carol told me she wished she had made that call a year earlier. Not because anything would have been prevented — Ruth's trajectory was what it was. But because having support in place changed the quality of the time they had, for both of them.

This chapter is about the options Carol found. Most families don't know they exist until they're already in crisis, or until a friend happens to mention the right thing at the right moment. You don't need to wait for that moment.

The Space Between Home and a Facility

One of the most common misconceptions about long-term care planning is that it involves a single binary decision: either your loved one lives at home, or they move to a facility. In reality, there is meaningful middle ground, a range of services and supports that can extend the time someone is safely able to remain at home, ease the burden on family caregivers, and improve the quality of the eventual transition when it comes.

These are not alternatives to placement. For most families, the trajectory toward some form of residential care is real and will eventually need to be addressed. What these options offer is something different: time, support, and the ability to approach a major decision from a position of preparation rather than exhaustion.

There are five categories worth understanding: in-home care, adult day programs, respite care, hospice and palliative care, and geriatric care managers. Each serves a different purpose. Used well, and often in combination — they can meaningfully change the experience of the months or years leading up to a placement decision.

> *The families who use these options most effectively are the ones who find them before they desperately need them, not the ones who discover them in the middle of a crisis.*

In-Home Care

What It Is

In-home care is exactly what it sounds like: paid caregivers who come to the home to provide assistance with daily life. It ranges from companion care — someone to provide company, help with meals, and assist with light tasks — to personal care, which includes help with bathing, dressing, grooming, and mobility. At the more clinical end, home health agencies can provide skilled nursing visits, physical or occupational therapy, wound care, and medication management under a physician's order.

In-home care can be arranged through a home care agency, which handles hiring, background checks, scheduling, and backup coverage, or through independent caregivers hired privately. Agencies cost more but provide more structure and accountability. Private arrangements can be more flexible but carry more responsibility for the family in terms of oversight and logistics.

What It Does Well

At its best, in-home care preserves independence and routine while filling the gaps that have become safety concerns. It gives family caregivers relief — scheduled hours when they know their loved one is cared for and they can attend to their own lives. It also provides an outside set of eyes: a good home care aide will notice changes in condition, behavior, or environment that family members, adjusted to the gradual baseline shifts described in Chapter Two, may no longer see clearly.

What to Know Before You Start

Home care is primarily a private-pay service. Medicare covers skilled home health services under specific conditions — following a hospitalization or when a physician certifies a homebound status and a need for skilled care, but it does not cover ongoing companion or personal care. Medicaid covers home care services in many states through waiver programs, though eligibility and availability vary widely. Long-term care insurance policies often include home care benefits, which is one of the reasons having that coverage in place before it is needed matters so much.

The cost of in-home care varies widely by region and level of service, but families should expect it to be meaningful. Twenty hours a week of home care can approach or exceed the cost of assisted living in some markets, which is a conversation worth having with a financial planner before committing to a long-term arrangement. Chapter Five covers the financial picture in full.

> *If your loved one is resistant to the idea of having someone in the home, and many are — starting small helps. A few hours a week framed as 'help around the house' rather than 'care' can ease the transition in ways that a direct conversation about needing assistance sometimes cannot.*

Adult Day Programs

What They Are

Adult day programs, sometimes called adult day services or adult day health centers — provide structured care and programming in a community setting during daytime hours, typically weekdays. Participants come for the day and return home in the evening. Programs vary in their focus: some are primarily social, offering activities, meals, and companionship for adults who are relatively independent but isolated. Others are health-focused, with nursing oversight, medication management, physical therapy, and programming specifically designed for participants with dementia or other cognitive impairments.

What They Do Well

Adult day programs address two needs simultaneously. For the person attending, they provide stimulation, social connection, structured activity, and in health-focused programs, professional monitoring. Research consistently shows that social engagement and cognitive stimulation can slow the progression of dementia, which is one of the reasons memory care facilities that do this well produce better outcomes than those that don't. An adult day program can deliver some of those same benefits while a person is still living at home.

For the caregiver, adult day programs provide something equally valuable: predictable, reliable time off. The psychological relief of knowing that your loved one is safe, engaged, and supervised for a defined block of hours — hours you can use to work, rest, run errands, or simply breathe — is not a luxury. It is a sustainability measure. Caregivers who have structured respite built into their week last longer and provide better care than those who don't.

What to Know Before You Start

The cost of adult day programs is generally lower than in-home care and much lower than residential care. Medicaid covers adult day services in many states, and some long-term care insurance policies include coverage. Veterans' benefits may also apply for eligible individuals. Programs vary considerably in quality — visiting in person, observing the environment and the staff's interaction with participants, and asking about programming specific to your loved one's needs will tell you far more than a brochure will.

Transportation is worth asking about early. Some adult day programs provide or coordinate transportation for participants, which can be a deciding factor for families where getting to and from the program is a logistical challenge. Where transportation is not provided, home care agencies, community organizations, and local Area Agencies on Aging can often help identify options.

Resistance is common here too. Many adults, particularly those who don't fully recognize their own decline, resist the idea of a program they perceive as designed for people worse off than they are. A trial visit — framed as trying something new rather than a permanent arrangement, often works better than a direct conversation about need. Ruth's initial reaction to the day program Carol enrolled her in was resistance. Within three weeks, she was telling Carol about the friends she'd made there.

Respite Care

What It Is

Respite care refers to short-term, temporary care designed to give family caregivers a break. It can take several forms: in-home respite through a home care agency, a short-term stay at an adult day program, or — most useful for planning purposes, a temporary residential stay at an assisted living community or skilled nursing facility. These short-term residential stays, sometimes called respite stays, typically last anywhere from a few days to a few weeks.

What It Does Well

Respite care serves the caregiver first, and the person receiving care second, and there is no apology needed for that ordering. A caregiver who takes a planned break returns with more capacity than one who pushes through to the point of collapse. The research on caregiver burnout is unambiguous: sustained caregiving without relief produces serious health consequences for the caregiver, which ultimately compromises the quality of care the loved one receives. Respite is not a luxury or an indulgence. It is a clinical recommendation.

For families considering eventual placement, a respite stay serves an additional function: it gives the person receiving care a chance to experience a facility environment before a permanent transition is required. Families frequently report that a loved one who was deeply resistant to the idea of a facility came away from a respite stay with a different perspective — having experienced the social engagement, the structured meals, the activities, and the professional care in a context that wasn't permanent and wasn't a crisis.

What to Know Before You Start

Availability of short-term respite stays varies by facility and by care setting. Not all assisted living communities offer them, and skilled nursing facilities that do often have limited dedicated respite beds. Calling ahead and understanding what a facility offers, and at what cost — is an important step. Medicare covers short-term skilled nursing respite care under specific conditions for hospice patients. For most other situations, respite stays are private pay, though some long-term care insurance policies include respite benefits.

> *A respite stay at a facility you are seriously considering for eventual placement is one of the most useful evaluative tools available to a family. It tells you things about a facility that a tour never will.*

Hospice and Palliative Care

What They Are

Hospice and palliative care are related but distinct, a distinction that matters and that families often don't fully understand until they need to.

Palliative care is specialized medical care focused on relieving the symptoms, pain, and stress of serious illness. It can be provided alongside curative treatment, at any stage of illness, in any setting — at home, in a hospital, or in a care facility. It is not about giving up on treatment. It is about ensuring that the person's comfort and quality of life are being actively managed alongside whatever else is happening medically.

Hospice care is palliative care for people who are nearing the end of life — generally defined as a prognosis of six months or less if the illness follows its expected course. Hospice shifts the goal of care from cure to comfort, and provides a comprehensive team — physicians, nurses, social workers, chaplains, and home health aides — focused entirely on the quality of the person's remaining time. Hospice can be provided at home, in a facility, or in a dedicated hospice residence.

Why This Belongs in a Planning Conversation

Families often resist hospice because it feels like surrender — like acknowledging that there is nothing more to be done. What I have observed, consistently, is the opposite. Families who engage hospice services at the appropriate time typically report that it gave their loved one better care, more comfort, and more dignity in the final chapter than they would have received otherwise. And it gave the family support — practical, emotional, and clinical, that they did not know was available to them.

The conversation about hospice belongs in any planning discussion where the trajectory of a diagnosis has shifted toward end of life. It is not a decision to be made in a crisis if it can be made thoughtfully before one. A frank conversation with your loved one's physician about whether hospice or palliative care is appropriate, or may become appropriate — is one of the most important conversations a family can have.

As with the other topics in this book, I am not a medical professional, and the decision about hospice is one that belongs with your loved one's care team. What I can tell you is that the families I have watched handle this well are the ones who had the conversation early enough to make a real choice, not the ones who arrived at hospice at the last possible moment because nobody had raised it sooner.

Geriatric Care Managers

What They Are

A geriatric care manager, also called an aging life care professional, is a specialist, typically with a background in social work, nursing, or gerontology, who helps families navigate the complexities of caring for an aging loved one. They assess the person's needs, develop a care plan, coordinate services, monitor changes in condition over time, and serve as an experienced guide through exactly the kind of territory this book is trying to describe.

Carol's call to a geriatric care manager is what changed the trajectory of her mother's final years. Not because the care manager did anything magical, but because she knew what questions to ask, what options existed, and how to put together a plan that Carol, without that knowledge, would not have been able to construct on her own.

What They Do Well

Geriatric care managers are particularly valuable in three situations: when a family is overwhelmed and doesn't know where to start, when family members are geographically dispersed and coordination is difficult, and when a loved one's needs are complex enough that managing them requires expertise the family doesn't have. They can serve as the family's eyes and ears when the family cannot be present — visiting facilities, monitoring the quality of in-home care, and flagging changes before they become crises.

They are also, for many families, the person who finally names what everyone has been circling around. An outside professional who can say, clearly and without the emotional freight of a family relationship: here is what I see, here is what the options are, here is what I would recommend — can move a family forward in ways that months of internal conversation sometimes cannot.

What to Know Before You Start

Geriatric care management is a private-pay service and is not covered by Medicare or most insurance. Fees vary by region and by the scope of services. Some families engage a care manager for a single comprehensive assessment and recommendation. Others use them on an ongoing basis as a coordinator and monitor. The Aging Life Care Association maintains a directory of credentialed professionals organized by location, which is a useful starting point for families who want to find someone qualified in their area.

> *If you are a family member reading this from a distance —
> managing a parent's care from another city or state, a
> geriatric care manager is one of the most valuable
> investments you can make. They become the local presence
> you cannot be.*

Using These Options Together

The most effective use of these bridge options is not choosing one and treating it as a solution. It is understanding them as a toolkit — complementary supports that can be combined and adjusted as a person's needs evolve.

A typical progression might look something like this: a geriatric care manager assesses the situation and recommends in-home care three days a week and an adult day program on the other two. As the person's needs increase, in-home care hours expand. A respite stay at a facility the family is considering gives everyone, including the person receiving care, a chance to experience what residential care actually looks and feels like. When the time for a permanent transition arrives, the family has already done much of the research, the person is familiar with the environment, and the decision is made from a position of knowledge rather than panic.

That is the version of this process that can provide a substantial quality outcome. It requires starting early enough that each step has time to be evaluated and adjusted. It requires willingness to ask for help, from professionals, from community resources, from each other — before the need becomes acute. And it requires letting go of the idea that managing everything independently is the measure of how much you love someone.

The measure is whether the person you love is receiving the right care, from people equipped to provide it, in a way that preserves their dignity and their quality of life for as long as possible. These options exist to help you do that. Use them.

Key Takeaways from Chapter Three

There is real middle ground between living at home without support and moving to a residential care facility. Most families don't know these options exist until they need them urgently.

In-home care provides help with daily activities and personal care in the home, ranging from companion care to skilled nursing visits. It is primarily private pay, though Medicaid waiver programs and long-term care insurance may apply.

Adult day programs provide structured care and programming in a community setting during daytime hours — benefiting both the person attending and the caregiver who gets reliable time off. Social engagement and stimulation in a quality program can slow cognitive decline.

Respite care, including short-term residential stays — gives caregivers planned relief and can give families a valuable preview of a facility they are considering for eventual placement.

Hospice and palliative care should not be seen as a form of surrender. Families who engage these services at the appropriate time consistently report better outcomes — more comfort, more dignity, more support — than those who wait or avoid the conversation.

Geriatric care managers are professional coordinators who can assess needs, build care plans, and serve as a local presence for families managing care from a distance. For complex situations, they are often the most valuable single investment a family can make.

These options work best in combination and when engaged before a crisis makes them reactive rather than proactive.

ACTION STEP:

Look at the current caregiving situation honestly and identify which of the five options in this chapter might address the most pressing gap, whether that is caregiver relief, daily support, clinical monitoring, or the need for an outside perspective. If you don't know where to start, a single call to a geriatric care manager is often the fastest way to get oriented. Add what you find to the When Readiness Checklist.

Now that you understand the options available before a placement decision, we turn to the medical picture. Chapter Four, Health, Diagnosis, and the Care Decision, walks through the specific conditions that most commonly drive placement decisions, what each one means for the level of care required, and how to have a productive conversation with a physician about what is coming.

CHAPTER FOUR

Health, Diagnosis, and the Care Decision

LEARNING TO READ THE MAP

When James's father was diagnosed with Parkinson's disease, James did what a lot of people do: he looked it up. He spent an evening reading about symptoms and medications, closed the laptop feeling vaguely informed, and then got on with his life. The diagnosis was real, but it felt manageable. His father was still driving. Still doing the crossword every morning. Still his father.

What James did not look up, what it did not occur to him to look up, was the trajectory. What Parkinson's disease actually looks like over five years. Over ten. What the progression means for daily functioning, for fall risk, for swallowing, for cognition. What level of care it eventually requires, and roughly when. Not because he was avoiding it, but because nobody had suggested that this was information worth having while his father was still doing the crossword.

Three years later, his father's mobility had declined significantly. He had fallen twice. He was having trouble with meals. James's mother, who had been managing everything quietly, mentioned one evening that she was tired in a way that frightened her. James realized he had no idea what came next — what the options were, what his father's specific situation meant for the type of care he would need, or how much time they had to figure it out.

He wasn't too late. That is the important thing. He was not standing in a hospital corridor with a 72-hour deadline. He had time, not unlimited time, but enough. Enough to have the conversations, ask the right questions, and make a plan that his father could still participate in.

What he needed was the map he hadn't thought to ask for three years earlier. This chapter is that map. It will not tell you what will happen to your loved one — medicine is not that precise, and the variations within any diagnosis are real. What it will give you is a way of understanding what a diagnosis typically means for the care decisions ahead, and how to have the conversations with your loved one's medical team that will help you fill in the specifics.

Why Diagnosis Matters for Planning

Not all health decline follows the same path. Some conditions progress slowly and predictably over years. Others plateau for long periods and then shift suddenly. Some are primarily physical in their impact on daily functioning; others affect cognition, behavior, or both. Understanding the general shape of a diagnosis — its likely trajectory, its typical care implications, and the points at which most families find themselves needing to make major decisions — is one of the most useful things a family can do early in the process.

This matters for several reasons. It allows you to anticipate rather than react. It helps you understand which type of care setting is likely to be appropriate at different stages — so you are researching the right category of options, not the wrong one. It gives you a basis for the conversations you need to have with your loved one's physicians. And it helps you recognize the signals from Chapter Two in context — understanding not just that something has changed, but what that change means for where you are on the road.

> *A diagnosis is not a verdict. It is information. And information, used well and early, is one of the most powerful planning tools a family has.*

A note before we go further: I am not a medical professional, and nothing in this chapter should be taken as medical advice or as a substitute for the guidance of your loved one's own physicians and care team. What follows is a guide drawn from decades of working with families navigating these diagnoses — intended to help you ask better questions and understand the answers, not to replace the clinical conversation that only your loved one's doctors can have with you.

Five Diagnoses and What They Mean for Care Planning

Alzheimer's Disease and Other Dementias

The General Trajectory

Alzheimer's disease and other dementias, including vascular dementia, Lewy body dementia, and frontotemporal dementia — are progressive conditions with no current cure. The trajectory is not linear: there are often periods of relative stability interrupted by periods of more rapid change, and the pace varies widely from person to person. But the direction does not vary. Over time, all forms of dementia involve increasing impairment in memory, cognition, behavior, and eventually the physical functions of daily life.

Early-stage dementia is often manageable at home with support, the kinds of bridge options described in Chapter Three. Middle-stage dementia, which typically brings significant memory loss, behavioral changes, increasing safety risks including wandering, and the need for substantial daily supervision, is often the point at which families find themselves facing a placement decision. Late-stage dementia almost universally requires skilled nursing-level care.

Care Planning Implications

Memory care is the care setting specifically designed for people with dementia, but as Chapter One described, the quality and programming of memory care varies enormously. For families navigating a dementia diagnosis, the planning work is not just about when, but about which facility, and that evaluation takes time and specific knowledge that Chapter Six will equip you with.

The behavioral dimension of dementia deserves particular attention. Agitation, aggression, sundowning, paranoia, and wandering are not simply symptoms to be managed — they are signals about the person's experience of their environment and their own confusion. A memory care program that is equipped to support someone through these stages looks very different from one that simply provides secure housing. Asking specific questions about how behavioral symptoms are managed is one of the most important things a family can do when evaluating a memory care program.

A Note on How to Communicate

One of the things families struggle with most, and that good memory care staff are specifically trained in — is how to communicate with someone whose sense of reality has shifted. The instinct is to correct: to remind, to reorient, to tell the truth. In most situations in life, that instinct serves us well. In dementia care, it often causes unnecessary pain.

Consider a resident who asks repeatedly when her husband is coming to visit, not knowing, or not retaining, that he passed away years ago. Telling her the truth does not give her information she can hold onto. It gives her grief — fresh, each time, that she will experience without the context that might soften it, and that she will have no memory of having already processed. The same question will come again. And the grief will come again with it.

The approach that experienced dementia care practitioners use is sometimes called validation therapy or therapeutic communication, the practice of entering the person's reality rather than insisting they return to yours. A response like "He'll be here soon" or "Tell me about him" redirects without confronting, soothes without deceiving in any way that harms. It is not a lie in the spirit of the word. It is an act of care, one that prioritizes the person's emotional experience over a factual correction they cannot use.

This approach takes practice and feels counterintuitive at first, especially for family members who have spent decades in an honest relationship with the person in front of them. It is worth learning, and worth asking about specifically when evaluating a memory care program. Staff who understand and practice this approach consistently produce calmer, more connected interactions with residents. Staff who don't often produce the opposite.

> *For families dealing with a dementia diagnosis: the window in which your loved one can meaningfully participate in decisions about their own care closes over time. Having those conversations — about wishes, about values, about what matters most — while that window is still open is one of the most important things early-stage planning makes possible.*

Parkinson's Disease

The General Trajectory

Parkinson's disease is a progressive neurological condition that primarily affects movement — causing tremor, rigidity, slowed movement, and balance problems that increase fall risk over time. But Parkinson's is more than a movement disorder. Many people with Parkinson's eventually experience cognitive changes, including a form of dementia that affects a significant portion of those with the disease. They may also experience sleep disturbances, depression, anxiety, swallowing difficulties, and autonomic symptoms that affect blood pressure, digestion, and bladder function.

The trajectory of Parkinson's is highly variable. Some people live relatively independently for many years after diagnosis with good medication management. Others decline more quickly. The presence of cognitive symptoms, falls, or swallowing difficulties generally signals a more advanced stage and more urgent care planning need.

Care Planning Implications

Parkinson's often requires a higher level of physical assistance than the diagnosis initially suggests. Fall risk is a serious concern and escalates as the disease progresses, a person with Parkinson's who falls once is at significantly elevated risk of falling again, with serious injury potential. The physical demands of caring for someone with advanced Parkinson's — helping with transfers, mobility, and personal care — frequently exceed what a solo family caregiver can safely manage.

Swallowing difficulties, when they emerge, introduce both a safety risk and a nutritional concern that typically require skilled nursing oversight. Speech therapy is an important component of Parkinson's care that families often don't know to ask about. Facilities that specialize in Parkinson's care or have real experience with the disease exist and are worth specifically seeking out.

> *James's story is a Parkinson's story. His father was still doing the crossword when the diagnosis came. Three years later, the picture had shifted considerably. The distance between those two points, and what happened in between — is exactly the space that early planning is designed to fill.*

Stroke and Traumatic Brain Injury

The General Trajectory

Stroke and traumatic brain injury (TBI) differ from the other diagnoses in this chapter in an important way: they are events, not progressive diseases. The damage occurs at a specific moment, and the subsequent trajectory is defined primarily by the severity of the initial injury and the course of recovery.

After a stroke or TBI, most recovery occurs in the first weeks and months, the period during which rehabilitation is most intensive and the brain's plasticity is most active. Recovery can be substantial, partial, or minimal, depending on the nature and extent of the injury. For some people, recovery plateaus at a level of functioning that is manageable at home with support. For others, the residual deficits — in mobility, cognition, communication, or the ability to manage daily activities — require a higher level of ongoing care.

Care Planning Implications

The immediate post-stroke or post-TBI period almost always involves a skilled nursing facility for rehabilitation, the short-term skilled care described in Chapter One. The critical planning question for families in this situation is what comes after rehabilitation: where does the person go when the acute recovery phase ends?

For families who have not done any advance planning, this question arrives at a moment of genuine emotional and logistical stress. The discharge timeline from a skilled nursing rehab stay is real, and making a good long-term decision under that kind of pressure is exactly the situation this book is designed to help you avoid.

People who have experienced one stroke are also at elevated risk for a subsequent stroke. Families managing a post-stroke situation should understand this risk and factor it into their planning, not as a source of anxiety, but as a reason to have the next level of planning already in place.

Congestive Heart Failure and Cardiac Conditions

The General Trajectory

Congestive heart failure (CHF) is a chronic condition in which the heart is no longer pumping efficiently, leading to fluid buildup, shortness of breath, fatigue, and reduced ability to perform physical activity. Unlike many other conditions that drive placement decisions, CHF does not follow a simple downward slope. It is characterized by a pattern of relative stability punctuated by acute episodes — exacerbations that often result in hospitalization and that, over time, leave the person at a lower functional baseline than before.

This pattern — stability, then a hospitalization, then a new lower baseline — is important for families to understand, because it means the time to plan is during the stable periods, not in the aftermath of a crisis. Each hospitalization is a potential inflection point. The family that has already done the planning work arrives at that point with options. The family that has not arrives in crisis.

Care Planning Implications

CHF management requires careful medication adherence, daily monitoring of weight and fluid status, dietary compliance, and the ability to recognize and respond to symptoms that signal an exacerbation. As the disease advances and these management requirements become more complex, or as cognitive decline makes self-management unreliable, the level of oversight required increases accordingly.

Skilled nursing facilities are well-equipped to manage CHF — they have the nursing staff, the medication protocols, and the clinical oversight that complex cardiac management requires. For families dealing with an advanced CHF diagnosis, conversations with the cardiologist about disease trajectory and likely hospitalization patterns are an important part of planning. Understanding roughly where on the trajectory a person is helps families gauge how much time they likely have to make thoughtful decisions.

COPD and Respiratory Conditions

The General Trajectory

Chronic obstructive pulmonary disease (COPD) is a progressive lung condition that makes breathing increasingly difficult over time. Like CHF, it follows a pattern of gradual decline interrupted by acute exacerbations — episodes of significantly worsened breathing that often require hospitalization and that leave the person at a reduced functional baseline afterward.

Advanced COPD significantly limits physical activity and can make even basic daily tasks — bathing, dressing, moving between rooms — exhausting. Oxygen therapy, which many people with advanced COPD require, adds a layer of complexity to daily care. Anxiety and depression are common in people with advanced COPD, driven in part by the frightening experience of breathlessness and in part by the progressive loss of physical capability.

Care Planning Implications

The caregiving demands of advanced COPD are often underestimated by families, in part because the person may appear relatively well when at rest, and in part because the decline tends to be gradual enough to normalize. The combination of oxygen management, medication complexity, limited mobility, and the emotional weight of the disease creates a caregiving burden that frequently exceeds what families realize they are carrying until a crisis makes it visible.

Skilled nursing facilities and assisted living communities with experience managing respiratory conditions and oxygen-dependent residents are an important filter when evaluating options for someone with advanced COPD. Not all facilities are equally equipped to handle the clinical and equipment needs of this population, and asking specifically about this experience is a reasonable and important question during facility evaluation.

The five diagnoses covered here are among the most common drivers of care placement decisions, but they are not the full picture. Many families are dealing with conditions not covered in this chapter: multiple sclerosis, kidney disease, Huntington's disease, complications of diabetes, and others. The approach here — understanding trajectory, identifying the signals that mark transition points, and having the planning conversation with a physician before a crisis forces it — applies to any serious diagnosis. The specifics are best understood in conversation with your loved one's own care team, who can speak to the particular shape of their condition and what it means for the decisions ahead. Ask questions. Listen carefully. And don't leave without understanding what you've been told.

If You Want to Read More

Alzheimer's Disease and Other Dementias

The following books are consistently recommended by clinicians, social workers, and families navigating an Alzheimer's or dementia diagnosis. They range from practical caregiving guides to deeply human accounts of what this disease looks like from the inside.

The 36-Hour Day: A Family Guide to Caring for People Who Have Alzheimer Disease, Other Dementias, and Memory Loss — Nancy L. Mace and Peter V. Rabins

The most widely recommended book in dementia caregiving, often called the definitive guide. Now in its eighth edition, it covers daily challenges, behavioral changes, care settings, finances, and family dynamics with clarity and compassion. If you read one book, read this one.

Still Alice — Lisa Genova

A novel, but one written by a neuroscientist with a Harvard doctorate, and one of the most vivid accounts of early-onset Alzheimer's available. Genova's first-person narrative gives families a rare window into what the experience of cognitive decline feels like from the inside. Widely recommended by dementia care professionals for the understanding it builds.

Creating Moments of Joy Along the Alzheimer's Journey — Jolene Brackey

A practical and genuinely hopeful guide for caregivers focused on what is still present rather than what has been lost. Brackey's approach — celebrating small joys, adapting communication, finding meaning in each day — is grounded in real caregiving experience and consistently praised by families as one of the most useful books they found.

The Man Who Mistook His Wife for a Hat — Oliver Sacks

Not about Alzheimer's specifically, but perhaps the most illuminating book ever written about what it means to lose the ordinary functions of the mind and still remain, unmistakably, a person. Sacks' collection of neurological case studies — each one a small portrait of a human being living with a brain that has stopped working the way it should — gives families something no caregiving manual can: a genuine understanding of what their loved one's inner world may look and feel like. Essential, and unlike anything else on this list.

Parkinson's Disease

Parkinson's has a rich body of literature, both practical guides for families and more literary works that illuminate the human experience of the disease. The following are among the most frequently recommended.

Parkinson's Disease: A Complete Guide for Patients and Families — William J. Weiner, Lisa M. Shulman, and Anthony E. Lang
Published by Johns Hopkins University Press and written by leading neurologists, this is the most comprehensive medical reference available for families. It covers diagnosis, treatment options, medications, daily management, and long-term care planning in an accessible format. An authoritative starting point for any family navigating a Parkinson's diagnosis.

Living with Parkinson's Disease: A Complete Guide for Patients and Caregivers — Michael S. Okun, Irene A. Malaty, and Wissam Deeb
Dr. Okun is the National Medical Advisor of the Parkinson's Foundation and one of the country's leading Parkinson's researchers. This guide, now in its second edition, blends expert medical guidance with real-world experience — covering medications, therapies, the gut-brain connection, and a practical hospitalization safety guide for caregivers. Authoritative, current, and deeply practical.

Awakenings — Oliver Sacks
Not a caregiving manual — something rarer and more valuable. Sacks' account of his work with postencephalitic patients who developed Parkinsonian symptoms is a profound

meditation on what it means to be frozen and then to awaken, on the relationship between a physician and a patient, and on the humanity that persists inside a body that has stopped cooperating. Later adapted into a film starring Robert De Niro and Robin Williams. For anyone who wants to understand Parkinson's not just clinically but as a human experience, this is essential reading.

The Comfort of Home for Parkinson Disease: A Guide for Caregivers — Maria M. Meyer

A step-by-step practical guide for families providing care at home — covering daily challenges, fall prevention, safety adaptations, emotional support, and long-term planning. Illustrated, clearly written, and consistently recommended by neurology nurses and care professionals as the book they hand to families first.

The Conversation Most Families Don't Have — Until They Have To

Of all the planning failures I have observed over 34 years, one of the most consistent is this: families who have been living with a serious diagnosis for months or years and have never had a direct conversation with their loved one's physician about trajectory, prognosis, and care planning.

They have had plenty of appointments. They have discussed medications, test results, and symptom management. But the larger conversation, the one about where this is going, what it will eventually require, and what the family should be thinking about now — has simply never happened. Sometimes because the physician didn't initiate it. Sometimes because the family didn't know to ask. Often because both parties were focused on the immediate and no one made space for the longer view.

That conversation is worth having deliberately. Not in the five minutes at the end of a routine appointment, but as an appointment with a specific purpose. A family member asking to sit down with the physician, or the care team — specifically to discuss trajectory and planning is not an unusual request. Most physicians welcome it. Many are waiting for the family to ask.

Questions Worth Asking

The following questions are a starting point, not a script. Adapt them to your situation, your loved one's specific diagnosis, and what you most need to understand. The goal is not to get precise predictions, which medicine often cannot provide, but to develop a clearer picture of the road ahead.

What is the typical trajectory of this diagnosis, and where would you say my father/mother/spouse is on that trajectory right now?

What changes in condition or functioning should prompt us to reassess the current care situation?

Are there points in this disease's progression where most families find they need to consider a higher level of care? What does that typically look like?

What type of care setting is best suited to managing this condition as it progresses, and are there facilities or programs you would specifically recommend or that have experience with this diagnosis?

Is there anything about my loved one's specific presentation that you would want a care facility to know or to be specifically equipped for?

Are there conversations we should be having now — about advance directives, hospice eligibility, or goals of care, that we have not yet had?

If something were to change suddenly, a hospitalization, a significant decline — what would you want us to already have in place?

A note on advocacy: do not leave these appointments without understanding what you were told. If something is unclear, say so. Ask for it to be explained differently. Ask for written materials. Bring someone with you to take notes if that helps. The information from these conversations is too important to walk away from with a partial understanding, and no physician worth their time will think less of you for making sure you understand. Be your own advocate. Be an advocate for others.

What a Diagnosis Cannot Tell You

A diagnosis gives you a framework. It does not give you a timeline, and it does not tell you who your loved one is within that picture.

The same diagnosis can look very different in two people of the same age, depending on their overall health, their engagement with treatment, their social support, and factors that medicine does not fully understand. The signals in Chapter Two matter precisely because they are specific to your loved one, not to a statistical average of everyone with the same diagnosis. The trajectory information in this chapter is a map of the general terrain. The signals are where you are on it.

What diagnosis can tell you is when to start paying attention, what to pay attention to, and what conversations to have while you still have time to have them well. That is not a small thing. James's father still had good months ahead of him when James finally had the conversation he'd been circling. He was able to tell James which things mattered most to him — being near family, having access to a garden, not sharing a room. Information that shaped the search that followed, and that James would not have had if he'd waited for a crisis to ask.

> *The goal of this chapter is not to make a diagnosis feel more frightening than it is. It is to make it feel more navigable. Knowing the road ahead does not mean you have lost. It means you have time to choose your route.*

Key Takeaways from Chapter Four

A diagnosis is information, not a verdict. Understanding the general trajectory of a condition gives families the ability to anticipate care needs rather than react to them.

Different diagnoses have different shapes. Alzheimer's and other dementias progress continuously; CHF and COPD follow patterns of stability and acute episodes; Parkinson's involves both movement and cognitive dimensions; stroke and TBI involve recovery from a single event with an uncertain endpoint.

The behavioral dimension of dementia, agitation, wandering, paranoia, requires specifically equipped memory care. Not all memory care programs are equally prepared for advanced dementia. Asking specific questions about behavioral management is necessary.

Fall risk, swallowing difficulties, and cognitive changes are three signals that frequently mark a significant transition point in multiple diagnoses. When they appear, the care planning conversation becomes urgent.

The physician conversation about trajectory and care planning is one of the most important conversations a family can have, and one of the most commonly deferred. Requesting it deliberately, with a specific agenda, is the most effective way to have it.

A diagnosis cannot tell you who your loved one is within its structure. The signals from Chapter Two, combined with the trajectory information here, give you both the map and your current position on it.

ACTION STEP:

Using the questions in this chapter as a guide, have a dedicated conversation with your loved one's primary physician or specialist, not at the end of a routine appointment, but as a specific meeting to discuss trajectory and planning. If your loved one does not yet have a diagnosis but you are observing the signals from Chapter Two, this appointment is still worth having. Add what you learn to the When Readiness Checklist.

Understanding the medical picture matters. But for most families, the care decision is also shaped, and sometimes constrained — by financial reality. Chapter Five, The Financial Landscape of Long-Term Care, covers how long-term care is actually paid for: what Medicare covers and what it doesn't, how Medicaid works and what it requires, what long-term care insurance does, and what families who have done none of this planning yet can still do.

CHAPTER FIVE

The Financial Landscape of Long-Term Care

THE NUMBER NOBODY HAD PREPARED FOR

Patricia and her brother Tom had a stressful time arranging their mother's transfer from the hospital to a skilled nursing facility after her stroke. They had toured three facilities, chosen the one that felt right, and signed the admission paperwork with the particular exhaustion of people who have been making hard decisions for too long. The immediate crisis was over. Their mother was safe. They allowed themselves, briefly, to exhale.

The admissions team had walked them through the financial picture at intake — Medicare coverage, the co-payment that would apply after day twenty, what would happen through day one hundred. The information was all there. Patricia and Tom had nodded through the conversation the way people nod when they are absorbing more than they can hold at once, and then they had gone home to call their siblings and eat something and try to sleep.

What they had not fully understood, what most families don't, is that Medicare's skilled nursing benefit is a rehabilitation benefit.

It pays for recovery. Physical therapy. Occupational therapy. The skilled work of getting someone back to a functional baseline after an acute medical event. The average Medicare patient stays in a skilled nursing facility for two to three weeks. Most never approach day 100. Coverage continues as long as the patient is making measurable progress, and ends when progress plateaus, whether that is day 18 or day 45.

Their mother's stroke had left her with significant deficits. She was working hard in therapy. But two weeks in, the care team sat down with Patricia and Tom for a discharge planning conversation that neither of them had been prepared for. Their mother was not going to be ready to go home. Not soon, and possibly not at all, not to the home she had lived in, alone, before the stroke. The question on the table was not about rehabilitation anymore. It was about what came next. Long-term care. And Medicare, the team explained gently, would not pay for that.

Patricia and Tom had heard those words at intake. They had not understood, then, that they were the words that would matter most. They did not know about Medicaid. They did not know what their mother's assets would mean for eligibility. They did not know whether she had long-term care insurance — it took them some time to find the policy, buried in a filing cabinet, that turned out to cover exactly this situation.

The policy covered it. The ending was manageable. But the weeks of uncertainty between that discharge planning conversation and the discovery of the policy — weeks of genuine worry about whether they could afford the right care for their mother — were entirely preventable. Not because anyone had failed them. Because they had walked into the process without the foundation to understand what they were being told, and without knowing which questions to ask before they needed the answers.

This chapter is the financial conversation most families don't have until a situation forces it. It will not replace the guidance of a financial planner or elder law attorney, and for most families in a complex situation, that guidance is worth seeking. What it will do is give you the map: what the major payment sources are, what they cover, what they don't, and what the decisions you make now mean for the options you'll have later.

How Long-Term Care Is Actually Paid For

One of the most important things to understand about long-term care financing is that the primary payer is almost never who families expect it to be. Medicare, the program most older Americans know best — covers very little long-term care. The programs that cover the most are Medicaid, for those who qualify, and private pay — meaning the family's own assets, for everyone else.

The landscape has six main components worth understanding: Medicare, Medicaid, long-term care insurance, private pay and asset planning, veterans benefits, and the newer model of value-based care that is reshaping how some of this care is delivered and paid for. Each operates differently, covers different things, and requires different planning to access effectively.

> *The families who have the most options at the moment of a placement decision are almost always the ones who started the financial conversation before they needed to. The families with the fewest options are often those who assumed the system would take care of things, and discovered, too late, that it wouldn't.*

Medicare

What It Covers

Medicare is the federal health insurance program for Americans 65 and older and for certain younger people with disabilities. It covers a wide range of medical care — hospital stays, physician visits, outpatient services, prescription drugs, and it does cover short-term skilled nursing care under specific conditions.

To qualify for Medicare-covered skilled nursing care, three conditions must be met: the person must have had a qualifying hospital stay of at least three inpatient days, they must be admitted to the skilled nursing facility within 30 days of that hospital discharge, and they must require skilled services — meaning nursing care, physical therapy, occupational therapy, or speech therapy, that can only be provided in a skilled nursing setting.

When those conditions are met, Medicare covers the first 20 days of skilled nursing care in full. From day 21 through day 100, Medicare requires a fixed daily co-payment — an amount that adjusts annually and that most supplemental insurance policies cover. After day 100, Medicare coverage ends entirely for that benefit period.

The Critical Limits Families Miss

COMMON MYTH: *"Medicare will cover the nursing home."*

THE REALITY: Medicare covers short-term skilled nursing care — rehabilitation after a qualifying hospital stay — under specific conditions and for a limited time. It does not cover long-term custodial care: the ongoing nursing supervision, personal care, and daily support that most people in skilled nursing facilities on a long-term basis actually need. This distinction is one of the most consequential misunderstandings in long-term care planning.

COMMON MYTH: *"She gets 100 days — Medicare will cover her through day 100."*

THE REALITY: The 100-day maximum is a ceiling, not a guarantee. Medicare requires ongoing documentation that the patient is making measurable progress toward recovery. If progress plateaus, as it often does in long-term conditions — Medicare coverage can end well before day 100. Families who are counting on a full 100 days of coverage are frequently surprised when coverage ends at day 30, 45, or 60.

It is also worth understanding how Medicare benefit periods work when a person is discharged and then requires skilled nursing care again. A benefit period ends only after a person has been out of inpatient hospital or skilled nursing facility care for 60 consecutive days. Any readmission before that 60-day mark, whether it occurs on day 5, day 30, or day 59 — keeps the person in the same benefit period, and Medicare skilled nursing coverage continues from where it left off. Only after a full 60-day break does a new benefit period begin — resetting the coverage clock, including a new 20-day fully covered period. These rules are important to understand if your loved one's situation involves multiple hospitalizations or transitions. Because Medicare rules can change and individual situations vary, always confirm the specific benefit period status with the facility's billing team or a Medicare counselor.

Medicare Advantage plans, the private insurance alternative to traditional Medicare — may offer different skilled nursing benefits than original Medicare, sometimes more generous and sometimes more restrictive. If your loved one is enrolled in a Medicare Advantage plan, understanding the specific skilled nursing benefits of that plan before a placement is needed is an important step. The rules can differ sharply from traditional Medicare, and the network of covered facilities may be limited.

Medicaid

What It Is and What It Covers

Medicaid is the joint federal-state program that provides health coverage for people with limited income and assets. Unlike Medicare, Medicaid does cover long-term custodial care, the ongoing skilled nursing care that Medicare will not pay for. It is, in fact, the largest single payer of long-term care in the United States. For families whose loved ones require extended skilled nursing care and who do not have long-term care insurance or sufficient private assets to self-fund, Medicaid is often the program that ultimately pays the bill.

But Medicaid eligibility comes with significant conditions. It is means-tested — meaning it requires that a person's income and assets fall below specific thresholds, which vary by state. A person with substantial assets is not immediately eligible for Medicaid; they must first spend those assets down to the allowable limits before Medicaid will begin paying. This process, and the planning strategies available to navigate it — is where the complexity lies.

Spend-Down and Common Misconceptions

COMMON MYTH: *"We'll just spend down and then Medicaid will cover everything."*

THE REALITY: Spend-down is real, but it is not as simple as depleting assets and applying. Medicaid has a look-back period, typically five years, during which it reviews asset transfers. Gifts to family members, property transfers, or other financial moves made within that window can result in a period of Medicaid ineligibility. Planning done well in advance of need can protect assets legally and legitimately. Planning done in crisis, after the need has arrived, has far fewer options.

COMMON MYTH: *"Medicaid will pay for any facility."*

THE REALITY: Medicaid only covers care in facilities that accept Medicaid, and not all do. This is a planning consideration, not a quality statement: many excellent skilled nursing operators accept Medicaid and provide outstanding care. But some facilities, particularly certain private-pay communities, do not participate in Medicaid at all, and others have limited Medicaid beds with waiting lists. A family whose plan is to rely on Medicaid should research which facilities in their area accept it and understand at what point in a stay Medicaid would become the payer — so that facility choices are made with a full picture of the options.

Medicaid rules are complex, highly state-specific, and change frequently. For families who believe Medicaid may be part of their long-term care financing picture, either now or in the future — consultation with an elder law attorney who specializes in Medicaid planning is one of the most valuable investments they can make. The strategies available to families who plan five or more years in advance look very different from those available to families planning in the middle of a crisis.

Long-Term Care Insurance

What It Does

Long-term care insurance is private insurance specifically designed to cover the costs of long-term care services, including home care, adult day programs, assisted living, memory care, and skilled nursing facility care. Policies vary considerably in their benefits, but most provide a daily or monthly benefit amount that offsets the cost of care for a defined benefit period, after a waiting period (the elimination period) during which the policyholder pays out of pocket.

A good long-term care insurance policy can be one of the most financially valuable assets a family has at the moment of a placement decision. Patricia and Tom's mother had one, and finding it changed their situation entirely. The families who don't have one, or who don't know they have one, or whose policy lapsed years ago without anyone noticing, face a fundamentally different financial picture.

Who Should Have It and When

Long-term care insurance is most effectively purchased in a person's 50s or early 60s, before health conditions that would disqualify coverage or significantly increase premiums have developed. The older a person is at application, the higher the premium, and beyond a certain point, coverage may be unavailable entirely due to health underwriting.

For families with aging parents who do not currently have coverage, the honest answer is that it may be too late for a traditional long-term care policy, but alternatives exist. Hybrid life insurance and annuity products with long-term care riders have become increasingly common and may be accessible to people who no longer qualify for traditional coverage. A financial planner with expertise in elder care planning can assess what options remain available.

If a Policy Exists — Find It

One of the most consistently overlooked steps in long-term care planning is simply locating any insurance policies that may exist. Older adults frequently have policies they purchased decades ago and have largely forgotten. Adult children often don't know whether a policy exists at all. Finding out — by looking through files, checking with former employers about group coverage, or reviewing bank statements for premium payments — is worth doing before a placement decision is made, not after.

If you do not know whether your loved one has long-term care insurance, finding out is one of the first things to do. The policy that changes everything may already exist. It just needs to be found.

Private Pay and Asset Planning

The Reality of Self-Funding

For families without long-term care insurance and with assets above Medicaid eligibility thresholds, the default payment method for long-term care is private pay — using savings, investments, retirement accounts, home equity, or other assets to cover the cost of care directly. This is how a large portion of long-term care is actually paid for in the United States, and it is worth understanding clearly what that means in practice.

The costs of long-term care are substantial. Assisted living communities typically range from $4,000 to $7,000 or more per month depending on location, level of care, and amenities. Skilled nursing facilities average higher, often $9,000 to $12,000 or more per month for a private room in many markets. Memory care, which typically commands a premium over standard assisted living, can approach or exceed skilled nursing costs in some areas. These figures vary widely by region and change over time, but the scale is important to understand before making placement decisions.

What Families Can Still Do

For families who have not done long-term care financial planning and are now facing an imminent need, the options narrow, but they do not disappear. Home equity is often the largest asset available, and options including home sale, reverse mortgage, or home equity lines of credit can be part of the funding picture. Annuities structured to fund long-term care costs may be available. Life insurance policies sometimes have long-term care riders or can be surrendered or sold. And a careful review of all assets with a financial planner experienced in elder care, done with appropriate urgency, can often identify options that are not immediately obvious to families going through this for the first time.

The earlier this conversation happens, the more options exist. That is the consistent truth of long-term care financial planning, and it applies to private pay as much as to Medicaid planning or insurance purchase. A family that begins the asset conversation five years before a placement is needed has meaningfully more flexibility than one that begins the week of admission.

Veterans Benefits

Aid & Attendance and Related Programs

Veterans and their surviving spouses may be eligible for benefits that can meaningfully offset long-term care costs — benefits that are consistently underutilized because families don't know they exist or don't understand the eligibility requirements.

The most significant is the VA's Aid & Attendance benefit, a pension enhancement available to wartime veterans and surviving spouses who require the regular assistance of another person for daily activities, are bedridden, or are residing in a nursing home due to physical or mental incapacity. The benefit provides a monthly payment that can be used for home care, assisted living, or skilled nursing costs. Eligibility is based on service history, need for care, and financial criteria, and the application process is detailed enough that working with a VA-accredited claims agent or elder law attorney is strongly recommended.

Beyond Aid & Attendance, the VA operates its own network of long-term care facilities and community living centers, and offers a range of community-based services including home care, adult day programs, and respite care for eligible veterans. The availability of these services varies by location and eligibility category.

> *If your loved one served in the military during a wartime period, veterans benefits should be part of any long-term care financial conversation. The Aid & Attendance benefit alone can provide meaningful monthly assistance. Start with the VA or a VA-accredited claims agent to understand what may be available.*

Value-Based Care: A Term Worth Understanding

What It Is

Value-based care is a term families increasingly encounter when dealing with Medicare Advantage plans, post-acute care networks, and facility admissions, and it can be confusing precisely because it is used to describe both a payment model and a philosophy of care.

At its core, value-based care is a shift away from the traditional fee-for-service model — in which providers are paid for the volume of services they deliver — toward a model in which providers are paid based on patient outcomes, quality measures, and cost efficiency. The theory is that aligning financial incentives with outcomes produces better care at lower cost. In practice, value-based arrangements take many forms, and the experience for patients and families varies considerably depending on how they are structured.

The 2030 Goal, and Why the SNF World Is Paying Attention

If you have spent any time around skilled nursing facilities or post-acute care providers in recent years, you have likely heard some version of this claim: that everyone will be in a Medicare Advantage plan by 2030. That claim is grounded in a real and meaningful policy commitment, but the precise framing matters, because the shorthand often blurs two distinct things.

In 2021, CMS formally established a goal of having 100 percent of Traditional Medicare beneficiaries in accountable care relationships by 2030 — meaning arrangements in which a provider or organization is responsible for both the quality and the total cost of that person's care. This is not the same as enrolling everyone in Medicare Advantage. It operates on a parallel track: beneficiaries can remain in traditional fee-for-service Medicare and still be in an accountable care relationship through an Accountable Care Organization, or ACO, a group of providers that coordinates care and shares in savings when costs come in below targets. As of early 2025, CMS reports that more than half of Traditional Medicare beneficiaries — over 14.8 million people — are already in such a relationship, the largest share ever recorded, and the pace of growth is accelerating.

At the same time, Medicare Advantage, the private alternative to traditional Medicare — has crossed the 50 percent enrollment threshold and is projected to cover roughly 64 percent of eligible beneficiaries by 2034. Both tracks are moving in the same direction. Whether a beneficiary is in traditional Medicare with an

ACO or in a Medicare Advantage plan, the financial logic surrounding their care is increasingly organized around outcomes and total cost rather than volume of services. Skilled nursing facilities are feeling pressure from both directions simultaneously, and that pressure is reshaping how post-acute care is delivered, evaluated, and paid for.

What It Means for Families

From a family's perspective, value-based care most commonly appears in two practical contexts. The first is insurance and plan structure. Families whose loved ones are on Medicare Advantage should understand their plan's network before a skilled nursing placement becomes necessary, not all facilities they might prefer will be covered, and prior authorization requirements can affect the timing of transitions. Families whose loved ones are in traditional Medicare may find that their primary care provider participates in an ACO, which can mean more coordinated care management and more structured transitions after a hospitalization or skilled nursing stay.

The second context is the facility itself. Skilled nursing facilities that participate in value-based programs, including CMS's various quality initiatives — are measured and rewarded based on metrics including readmission rates, functional outcomes, and patient satisfaction. Facilities that perform well on these measures are generally delivering better care. When evaluating facilities in Chapter Six, understanding how a facility performs on quality metrics, including those tied to value-based programs — is one of the most useful filters available to a family.

> *The practical takeaway: whether your loved one is on Medicare Advantage or traditional Medicare, the system*

surrounding their post-acute care is increasingly organized around accountability for outcomes. Knowing which arrangement applies, and what it means for facility choice, authorization, and care coordination — is worth understanding before a placement decision arrives.

The Financial Conversation With Aging Parents

For many families, the financial component of long-term care planning is delayed not because of lack of knowledge but because of discomfort. Talking about money with aging parents, especially about assets, insurance, and what happens when they can no longer manage their own affairs — touches on mortality, independence, and family dynamics in ways that make it easy to defer. And so it gets deferred, year after year, until a crisis makes it unavoidable under the worst possible conditions.

The conversation is worth having deliberately, while there is still time to act on what you learn. A few principles that help:

Frame it as planning, not crisis management. The conversation goes better when it is presented as something you are doing together, out of love and preparation, rather than as a response to a perceived decline. "I want us to understand the options while we have time to think about them carefully" is a different conversation than "We need to talk about what happens if something goes wrong."

Know what you are trying to find out. The key questions are: Does a long-term care insurance policy exist? What are the primary assets? Is there a will, a power of attorney, and a healthcare directive in place? Who are the financial and legal advisors? Where are the important documents kept? You do not need to cover everything in one conversation.

Involve the right professionals. A financial planner experienced in elder care planning and an elder law attorney are both worth engaging — ideally while your loved one is still able to participate in the planning. These professionals can identify options and strategies that families doing this without guidance routinely miss.

Do not wait for a crisis. The families who have the most options, and the least financial panic — at the moment of a placement decision are almost uniformly the ones who had this conversation before they needed to. It is an act of care for your loved one and for yourself.

> *The financial conversation is not about taking over. It is about understanding — so that when decisions need to be made, they can be made from a position of knowledge rather than fear.*

Key Takeaways from Chapter Five

Medicare covers short-term skilled nursing care under specific conditions, but not long-term custodial care. The 100-day maximum is a ceiling, not a guarantee. Understanding what Medicare actually covers before a placement is needed prevents one of the most common and costly financial surprises families face.

Medicaid covers long-term custodial care for those who qualify, but eligibility requires spending assets down to specific thresholds, and the five-year look-back period means that planning done in advance has far more options than planning done in crisis.

Long-term care insurance, if it exists, can be one of the most financially important assets a family has. Finding out whether a policy exists, and what it covers — should happen before a placement is needed, not after.

Private pay is how much of long-term care is actually funded. The costs are substantial and vary by setting, location, and level of care. A financial planner experienced in elder care can help families understand their options and protect assets where possible.

Veterans benefits, including the Aid & Attendance pension enhancement — are consistently underutilized. Any family with a wartime veteran should explore VA benefits as part of the long-term care financial picture.

Value-based care is reshaping how Medicare Advantage plans manage post-acute care and how facilities are measured for quality. Families with loved ones on Medicare Advantage should understand their plan's network and authorization requirements before a skilled nursing placement is needed.

The financial conversation with aging parents is best had early, framed as planning rather than crisis response, and supported by the right professional guidance. The families with the most options are almost always the ones who started this conversation before they needed to.

ACTION STEP:

Start with the essentials: find out whether a long-term care insurance policy exists, understand which Medicare coverage your loved one has (traditional or Medicare Advantage), and identify whether veterans benefits may apply. If you have not had the financial conversation with your loved one, this week is a good time to begin it. And if the financial picture is complex — substantial assets, Medicaid planning questions, no existing coverage, a consultation with an elder law attorney or elder care financial planner is worth scheduling before a placement decision arrives.

You understand the landscape, the signals, the bridge options, the medical picture, and the financial reality. Chapter Six, How to

Evaluate a Facility, gives you the practical tools to act on all of it — what to look for on a tour, what questions to ask, what the publicly available quality data actually tells you, and how to tell the difference between a facility that photographs well and one that actually delivers good care.

CHAPTER SIX

How to Evaluate a Facility

By the time most families are ready to tour a facility, they may have done the hardest parts: recognizing the signals, working through the financial picture, understanding the diagnosis. What they often have not done is learn how to evaluate what they are about to see.

This matters more than most families realize. A well-run facility and a poorly run one can look nearly identical on a tour. Both will have clean lobbies. Both will have friendly admissions staff. Both will show you the nicest available room and mention the activities calendar and the chef-prepared meals. The differences that actually predict the quality of care a person receives, the staffing culture, the quality metrics, the way a care aide interacts with a resident in a hallway when no one is watching — do not announce themselves. You have to know where to look.

This chapter gives you that. It is organized around the six dimensions of facility evaluation that matter most: the data you should review before you ever walk through the door, what to observe on the tour itself, how to read staff and culture, the questions worth asking administration directly, the red flags that should give you pause, and how evaluation differs by care setting. It closes with the When Readiness Checklist, the practical planning tool that every chapter in this book has been building toward.

A word before we begin: nothing in this chapter is meant as a criticism of the long-term care industry. I have spent 34 years working alongside operators, clinicians, and caregivers who are committed to their residents and who do extraordinary work in a demanding field. The sensationalism that sometimes surrounds this industry, the headlines that treat every long-term care facility as a cautionary tale — does a disservice both to the people who work in it and to the families who need to make clear-eyed decisions about it. Quality varies in long-term care as it varies in every industry. Most facilities are staffed by people who care. Some are better run than others. The tools in this chapter are not about finding reasons to be afraid. They are about helping you find the right place, and to know it when you see it.

> *The goal of facility evaluation is not to find a perfect place. It is to find the right place, the one whose strengths match your loved one's specific needs, whose culture you can trust, and whose quality you can verify. Those are learnable judgments. This chapter will teach you how to make them.*

Before You Tour: The Data

CMS Care Compare and the Five-Star Rating System

One of the most useful tools available to families evaluating skilled nursing facilities is the CMS Care Compare website — medicare.gov/care-compare, which publishes quality data on every Medicare- and Medicaid-certified nursing home in the country. Before you tour any facility, look it up.

Before reviewing the data, it helps to understand where it comes from. Every Medicare- and Medicaid-certified nursing facility in the country is subject to at least an annual health and safety inspection conducted by the state — an unannounced survey in which state surveyors review care practices, medication management, staffing, resident rights, and physical environment. Facilities can also be surveyed at any time in response to a formal complaint or concern. The results of these surveys, including any deficiencies cited and the facility's plan of correction — become part of the public record and feed directly into the data on CMS Care Compare. This oversight is rigorous and ongoing. It is the foundation on which the Five-Star system is built.

The Five-Star Quality Rating System rates facilities on three domains, each worth understanding separately:

Health Inspections — based on state survey findings from the most recent three years of annual inspections and complaint investigations. This is the most direct measure of regulatory compliance and safety. A low health inspection rating is a serious signal and warrants careful scrutiny. A high rating does not guarantee quality, but a poor one should not be dismissed.

Staffing — measures hours of care per resident per day for registered nurses, licensed nurses, and nurse aides, adjusted for the facility's case mix. Staffing levels are one of the strongest predictors of care quality in the research literature. Low staffing ratings often correlate with rushed care, missed assessments, and higher rates of preventable complications.

Quality Measures — tracks clinical outcomes including pressure ulcer/injury rates, fall rates with injury, antipsychotic medication use, hospital readmission rates, and functional decline measures. These are reported separately for short-stay and long-stay residents. Look at the measures most relevant to your loved one's specific condition and care needs.

The overall star rating is a composite — useful as a starting point but not sufficient on its own. A facility can have a high overall rating with a weak staffing domain, or a middling overall rating with excellent quality measures. Look at each domain individually, and look at the trend over time: a facility whose ratings have been improving is a different story from one whose ratings have been declining, even if the current number is the same.

> *A five-star overall rating does not mean a facility is right for your loved one. A three-star rating does not mean it is wrong. The stars are a starting filter, not a final answer. Use them to prioritize your research and focus your questions, not to make the decision for you.*

State Survey Reports

CMS Care Compare also links to the full text of state inspection reports, the actual findings from health and safety surveys. These are worth reading, or at minimum skimming, before a tour. They describe specific deficiencies cited at the facility, the severity of those deficiencies, and whether they were corrected. A citation for a minor administrative issue is different from a citation for neglect, abuse, or a pattern of medication errors. Understanding what the citations were, and how the facility responded, tells you more than the star rating alone.

Ownership and Financial Stability

Who owns and operates a facility is a legitimate factor in evaluation. Ownership changes, private equity involvement, and history of regulatory sanctions are all publicly searchable. A facility that has changed ownership multiple times in a short period, or that is part of a chain with a poor regulatory track record in other markets, is worth examining more carefully. This is not a disqualifier — many large operators run excellent facilities, but it is context worth having.

The Tour: What to Look For Beyond the Surface

Arrive a little early, or a little late, not because you are trying to catch anyone off guard, but because the tour itself is a curated experience. The few minutes before your scheduled time, or the walk to the parking lot afterward, are often when you see the facility operating outside the presentation. Pay attention to what you notice.

The Residents

The residents are one of the most important things to observe on any tour. Look at whether they appear comfortable, engaged, and treated with dignity. Are residents in common areas interacting with staff and each other, or parked in hallways in wheelchairs without engagement? Do staff address residents by name? Do they make eye contact, pause to speak with them, touch them on the shoulder? The quality of ordinary interactions between staff and residents, not during a formal activity or a staged moment, but in passing — is one of the most reliable indicators of a facility's culture.

The Environment

Cleanliness matters, but it is also the easiest thing to prepare for a tour. Look beyond the lobbies and the model rooms. Ask to see a standard room, a hallway bathroom, and the dining room during a meal or shortly after. These are harder to stage. Notice whether the environment feels lived-in and maintained versus neglected. Notice whether call lights in hallways are being answered promptly. Notice whether residents' personal spaces — photographs, belongings, small dignifying touches — are present and respected.

The Dining Experience

Meal times are a window into a facility's operation. If you can observe a meal service, or better yet, arrange to have a meal during your visit — pay attention to how food is served, how long residents wait, whether staff are present and attentive, and whether residents who need assistance are actually receiving it in a timely and respectful way. Ask about meal flexibility: can residents choose what they eat, when they eat, and where they eat? The answers reveal how the facility balances operational efficiency with resident autonomy.

The Activities Program

Ask to see the activities calendar, not a printed brochure, but the actual current week's schedule. Is programming happening throughout the day and on weekends, or is it clustered in a few convenient blocks? Are activities varied and designed for different ability levels and interests? For memory care specifically, ask how programming is adapted for residents at different stages of cognitive impairment. A facility that answers this question with specificity and enthusiasm is a different facility from one that gestures vaguely at a whiteboard. And if an activity is scheduled during the time of your tour, look for it. Is it actually happening? A program that exists on paper but not in practice is telling you something about the gap between what a facility presents and what it delivers.

Staff: The Most Important Variable

The research on long-term care quality is consistent on one point above all others: staffing levels and staff culture are the strongest predictors of resident outcomes. A beautiful building with inadequate or poorly supported staff will deliver worse care than a modest building with a stable, well-trained, engaged team. This is the variable that matters most, and it is also the one that is hardest to assess from a tour alone, which is why asking the right questions is essential.

Staffing Ratios

Ask directly: what are the nurse-to-resident ratios on each shift, including nights and weekends? What is the aide-to-resident ratio? How does the facility handle staffing when a scheduled employee calls out? Facilities with strong staffing practices will answer these questions specifically and without defensiveness. Vague answers — 'we always make sure residents are taken care of' — are not answers. They are deflections, and they are worth noting.

Cross-reference what you are told against the CMS staffing data you reviewed before the tour. A facility that tells you it has excellent staffing but whose CMS data shows staffing levels below state and national averages deserves a follow-up question.

Turnover

Staff turnover is one of the most telling metrics in long-term care and one of the least discussed in admissions conversations.

High turnover, particularly among direct care aides, disrupts the continuity and familiarity that residents depend on, especially those with cognitive impairment. Ask what the annual turnover rate is for nursing aides and floor nurses. Ask how long the director of nursing and the administrator have been in their roles. Leadership stability matters: a facility with a long-tenured leadership team has had time to build and sustain a culture. A facility on its third administrator in two years has not.

How Staff Talk About Their Work

Pay attention to how the staff you encounter during a tour talk about their residents and their jobs. Do they speak about residents with warmth and specificity? Do they seem to know the residents they pass in the hallway? Is there a sense of purpose and connection in how they describe their work, or does the conversation feel transactional and rote? You cannot manufacture genuine care culture for a tour. When it is present, it is visible. When it is absent, that is visible too.

Smell, Culture, and the Intangibles

Experienced families and professionals who have evaluated many facilities over time consistently describe a set of impressions that are harder to quantify but no less real than the data. These deserve your attention.

The Smell Test — Literally

A facility that smells of urine or feces, not in a momentary way near a resident who has just been attended to, but pervasively and throughout common areas and hallways — is telling you something important about its incontinence care protocols and its standards for resident dignity. This is not a subtle signal. A well-run facility that takes dignity seriously manages incontinence promptly and respectfully. One that does not will smell like one that does not.

The Feel of the Place

Walk through the facility with a simple question in your mind: does this place feel like somewhere a person is living, or somewhere a person is being managed? The difference shows up in small things, whether hallways feel like corridors or like spaces where people spend time, whether the décor reflects the residents or the facility's marketing department, whether laughter is audible anywhere, whether the staff you pass seem harried or present. None of these things alone is decisive. Together, they tell you whether the culture of the place centers the residents or centers operations.

Your Own Reaction

Trust your instincts, but interrogate them. If something feels wrong and you cannot name it, try harder to name it before you dismiss the feeling. If something feels right, ask yourself what specifically is generating that impression, because 'it just felt warm' is less useful than 'I noticed every staff member I passed greeted residents by name and two of them stopped what they were doing to help a resident who seemed confused.' The instinct is data. The specifics are what matter.

Questions Worth Asking Administration

The admissions team is trained to show a facility at its best. That is their job, and it is not a criticism, but it means your questions need to go beyond what they are prepared to present.

The following questions are designed to move the conversation past the brochure.

What does a typical day look like for a resident at my loved one's level of care? Walk me through it from morning to evening.

How are care plans developed and how often are they reviewed? Who participates in that process, and how is the family involved?

What is your process when a resident's condition changes, either improves or declines? How is the family notified, and how quickly?

What is your staffing ratio on the overnight shift and on weekends? How do you handle call-outs? Do you use agency staff to fill open shifts, and if so, how often? Agency staff are contract workers hired through a staffing agency to fill gaps when regular employees are unavailable. While agency staffing is sometimes necessary, heavy reliance on it can disrupt the consistency and familiarity that residents depend on.

What is the annual turnover rate for your nursing aides? How long has your director of nursing been in this role?

How does the facility handle behavioral symptoms in residents with dementia? What is your approach to redirection and de-escalation?

What is your rehospitalization rate, and how does it compare to state and national averages?

What is your process for handling a family concern or complaint? Who do I contact, and what is the typical response time?

Are your physical, occupational, and speech therapists employed in-house, or do you contract with an outside therapy company? Is therapy offered seven days a week, or Monday through Friday only? For families whose loved ones are in a facility for rehabilitation, the answers matter: in-house therapists tend to be more integrated into the care team, and seven-day therapy schedules can meaningfully affect recovery timelines.

What happens if my loved one's financial situation changes — specifically, if they transition from private pay to Medicaid? Does the facility accept Medicaid, and is there a guaranteed bed?

Can I speak with a family member of a current resident as a reference?

That last question, asking for a family reference, is one that many families don't think to ask and that admissions staff don't offer. A facility confident in its care will be able to connect you with a willing family. One that cannot, or that hesitates meaningfully, has told you something.

Keep in mind: if you are taking a tour with someone who is not the Admissions Director or a member of the admissions or administration team, the person leading the tour may not have the same level of expertise. If needed and time allows, schedule a follow-up tour or a phone call with Admissions or Administration to get your questions answered fully.

Red Flags: When to Walk Away

Not every concern disqualifies a facility. Many issues have explanations, and context matters. But some things, observed during a tour or discovered in research, are serious enough to warrant either a direct conversation that produces a satisfying answer, or a decision to look elsewhere. These are those things.

RED FLAG: Staff ignore or talk over residents during the tour — speaking about a resident in their presence as if they are not there, or failing to acknowledge residents they pass in hallways.

RED FLAG: The facility cannot answer basic staffing questions specifically, or the answers conflict materially with CMS staffing data.

RED FLAG: A pervasive odor of urine or feces throughout common areas and hallways, not localized and momentary, but systemic.

RED FLAG: Recent state survey citations for abuse, neglect, or a pattern of medication errors, especially if the facility's response to your questions about them is defensive rather than transparent.

RED FLAG: Multiple ownership changes or leadership turnover in the past two years without a clear explanation — instability at the ownership and leadership level tends to flow downward to care quality.

RED FLAG: The facility cannot tell you what happens to your loved one's bed if they transition from private pay to Medicaid, or the answer is that there is no Medicaid option and no plan.

RED FLAG: Residents in common areas appear heavily sedated, disengaged, or uniformly parked without activity, engagement, or social interaction — particularly during daytime hours.

RED FLAG: The admissions team is unable or unwilling to connect you with a family reference, or discourages you from speaking with residents during the tour.

RED FLAG: Your instinct says something is wrong and, after trying to name it specifically, the specifics confirm the feeling.

RED FLAG: The tour feels rushed. A skilled nursing facility tour typically takes 45 minutes to an hour; an assisted living or memory care tour typically takes an hour or more. A facility that moves you through quickly, that does not linger, does not encourage questions, does not offer to show you more — may not be eager for close inspection. Time spent on a tour is a signal of confidence in what is being shown.

> *A red flag is not automatically a disqualifier, but it is always a question that deserves a clear answer. If the answer you receive is satisfying and specific, you can*

proceed with more confidence. If it is vague, defensive, or dismissive, that response is itself information about how the facility handles accountability.

Evaluating by Setting: AL, Memory Care, and SNF

The evaluation framework above applies broadly, but the emphasis shifts meaningfully depending on the type of care setting you are evaluating. Here is what to weigh most heavily in each.

Assisted Living

In assisted living, the central question is fit, whether the community's culture, programming, and level of service match your loved one's current needs and likely near-term trajectory. Assisted living communities vary enormously in what they provide: some offer a rich continuum with robust care services; others are primarily residential with limited clinical support. Understanding exactly what is included in the base rate and what triggers additional charges is essential — care level fees can add meaningfully to the monthly cost as needs increase.

Ask specifically about the facility's process when a resident's care needs exceed what the community can provide. What triggers a discharge? What support does the facility offer in finding the next level of care? A good assisted living community will have a transparent and thoughtful answer to this question. One that evades it may be setting you up for a difficult and rushed transition later.

Memory Care

Memory care evaluation requires the most specific and probing questions of any setting. Beyond the general approach, focus particularly on:

The physical environment — is it designed for wandering safety with secured perimeters and circular pathways that allow free movement without dead ends? Is it visually calm and navigable, or overstimulating and confusing?

Staff training and consistency — are staff specifically trained in dementia care, including validation techniques and behavioral de-escalation? Is there dedicated memory care staff, or are staff rotated across units?

Programming — is cognitive and sensory stimulation built into the daily schedule at multiple points, or concentrated in one group activity per day? Is programming adapted for different stages of cognitive impairment, or one-size-fits-all?

Behavioral management — ask directly how the facility manages agitation, aggression, and sundowning. The answer should describe a person-centered approach involving environmental modification, redirection, and individualized response, not a reflexive reliance on sedating medications.

Skilled Nursing Facilities

For skilled nursing, the clinical dimension of evaluation carries the most weight. Beyond staffing ratios and quality metrics, focus on the facility's track record with the specific conditions your loved one has. A facility with strong experience managing Parkinson's disease, or CHF, or complex wound care, is a fundamentally different resource than a generalist facility, even if their overall star ratings are similar.

For families in the post-acute rehab context, ask specifically about therapy staffing and scheduling: how many therapy sessions per day, which days of the week therapy is offered, and what the discharge planning process looks like from day one. A facility that treats rehabilitation as the central purpose of the stay, not an add-on service — will have clear, specific answers.

The When Readiness Checklist

Every chapter in this book has pointed toward this tool. The When Readiness Checklist is not a scoring system or a decision algorithm. It is a structured summary of where a family stands across the dimensions that matter most in long-term care planning — designed to surface what is known, what is unknown, and what still needs to be done.

Use it as a living document. Complete what you can today, note what requires more information, and return to it as circumstances change. The goal is not to check every box before acting — it is to know clearly what you know, what you don't, and what the gaps in your preparation are.

PART ONE: SIGNALS AND READINESS

SAFETY SIGNALS

Recurring falls or fall risk identified

Wandering behavior present or at risk

Unsafe driving or driving has stopped

Evidence of burns, injuries, or near-misses at home

Medication management has become unreliable

FUNCTIONAL SIGNALS

Significant decline in ADLs (bathing, dressing, meals, mobility)

Weight loss or nutritional concerns identified

Home maintenance and hygiene declining

Driving or independent transportation no longer safe

COGNITIVE AND BEHAVIORAL SIGNALS

Memory loss affecting daily safety and functioning

Confusion, disorientation, or personality changes noted

Social withdrawal or loss of interest in prior activities

Diagnosis of dementia or cognitive impairment confirmed

CAREGIVER SIGNALS

Primary caregiver expressing exhaustion, fear, or overwhelm

Caregiver's own health being affected by caregiving demands

Family conflict over care responsibilities or decisions

Current care situation no longer sustainable

PART TWO: MEDICAL AND DIAGNOSIS PICTURE

Primary diagnosis and known secondary conditions documented

Trajectory conversation held with primary physician or specialist

Understanding of likely care level needed at each stage

Advance directive and healthcare proxy in place

Hospice or palliative care conversation held if appropriate

List of current medications and managing physicians compiled

PART THREE: FINANCIAL READINESS

INSURANCE AND BENEFITS

Long-term care insurance policy located and reviewed

Medicare coverage type confirmed (traditional or Advantage)

Medicare Advantage network and SNF benefits understood

Veterans benefits eligibility investigated if applicable

Medicaid eligibility and planning needs assessed

ASSETS AND PLANNING

Primary assets identified and documented

Elder law attorney or financial planner consulted

Power of attorney (financial) in place

Will and estate documents current

Location of all important financial documents known

PART FOUR: FACILITY RESEARCH

PRE-TOUR RESEARCH

CMS Care Compare reviewed for each facility being considered

Star ratings reviewed by domain (not just overall)

State survey reports reviewed for recent citations

Ownership and operational history researched

TOUR OBSERVATIONS

Resident interactions with staff observed

Common areas, dining room, and standard room visited

Meal service observed or meal arranged

Activities calendar reviewed — current week, not brochure

Smell and environment noted throughout facility

QUESTIONS ASKED

Staffing ratios for all shifts confirmed and cross-referenced

Turnover rates for aides and nursing leadership obtained

Care plan process and family involvement explained

Behavioral management approach (if memory care) discussed

Medicaid acceptance and bed guarantee clarified

Family reference requested and followed up

PART FIVE: LOGISTICS AND TRANSITION READINESS

Geographic location and proximity to family assessed

Transportation plan for family visits considered

Preference for private vs. semi-private room noted

Loved one's preferences and wishes documented

Transition plan discussed with current care providers

Admission process and timeline understood

Personal items and room preparation plan in place

Key Takeaways from Chapter Six

Review CMS Care Compare data, including star ratings by domain and state survey reports — before touring any facility. The data available publicly is extensive, free, and more reliable than any brochure.

On a tour, observe residents first. The quality of ordinary interactions between staff and residents, in passing, unrehearsed, is one of the most reliable indicators of a facility's culture.

Staffing levels and staff stability are strong predictors of care quality. Ask specific questions, get specific answers, and cross-reference what you are told against CMS data.

The smell of a facility, the feel of its culture, and your own specific observations are all legitimate data. Trust instincts that you can also name specifically.

Ask the eleven questions in this chapter directly. The quality of the answers tells you as much as the content.

Red flags are not automatic disqualifiers, but they require clear, specific responses, not deflection. A facility that handles accountability well in a tour conversation is more likely to handle it well in care.

Evaluation emphasis shifts by setting: fit and trajectory in assisted living, staff training and behavioral approach in memory care, clinical specialization and therapy structure in skilled nursing.

The When Readiness Checklist is a living document. Use it to track what you know, what you are still learning, and what gaps remain in your preparation.

ACTION STEP:

Pull up CMS Care Compare and look up any facility you are currently considering — or, if you are earlier in the process, look up two or three facilities in your area as a practice exercise. Review each domain separately, read at least one state survey report, and note what questions it raises. Then complete the sections of the When Readiness Checklist that you can complete today, and note which sections need more work.

You have the tools to evaluate a facility. Chapter Seven, The Conversation You've Been Avoiding, addresses the hardest part of this process for most families: talking directly with your loved one about what is coming. What to say, how to say it, what to do when they resist, and how to have a conversation that honors both the relationship and the reality.

CHAPTER SEVEN

The Conversation You've Been Avoiding

There is a conversation that most families need to have and very few actually do, at least not until the absence of it forces something worse. It is the conversation about what is happening, what is coming, and what the people who love your aging parent or spouse, or family member are going to do about it. It is the conversation that requires sitting down with the people you love most and saying things that are hard to say.

Most families avoid it for as long as they possibly can. Not because they are careless or unloving — quite the opposite. They avoid it because they love the person they are afraid to hurt, because they do not want to acknowledge what is changing, because the conversation feels like a door that, once opened, cannot be closed. They avoid it because they have watched someone they love begin to diminish and have quietly, desperately hoped that it would not get worse. And sometimes, for a while — it does not. And the conversation waits.

And then something happens. A fall. A call from a neighbor. A hospitalization. And the conversation that could have been had thoughtfully, on a Tuesday afternoon with coffee, while the person most affected was still fully present and able to participate in their own future, that conversation now has to happen in a hospital corridor, in a blur of exhaustion and fear, with a discharge planner waiting for an answer.

This chapter is about having the conversation before something urgent happens. It covers the hard conversations that surround long-term care planning: talking directly with your loved one about what is coming, dealing with the particular complexity of speaking with someone whose cognitive capacity is diminished, knowing what to do when the person you are speaking with refuses to hear it, managing the family dynamics that these conversations almost always surface, and knowing how to move forward when the conversation can no longer happen because the family waited too long.

> *The most compassionate thing a family can do for a loved one facing a care transition is to have the conversation while the loved one can still participate in it. This is not cruelty. It is the deepest form of respect — treating the person as someone whose voice matters, whose preferences count, and whose future belongs to them.*

Why We Avoid It, and What Avoidance Costs

Understanding why this conversation is so hard is the first step toward having it. The reasons are not weakness or negligence. They are deeply human, and almost universal.

We Are Afraid of Causing Pain

The most common thing families say when asked why they have not had this conversation is some version of: I don't want to upset her. I don't want him to think I'm giving up on him. I don't want to take away her hope. These are not small fears. The love behind them is real. But the assumption embedded in them, that the conversation itself causes pain — is usually wrong. The person you love almost always knows that something is changing. They are often more afraid in the silence than they would be in the conversation. What feels like protection frequently lands as isolation.

We Are Grieving

Long-term care conversations are, at their core, grief conversations. They require acknowledging loss — of independence, of the life the person had, of the future everyone had imagined. Avoidance is often not about protecting the loved one. It is about protecting ourselves from having to sit in that grief. This is understandable. It is also costly, because grief deferred does not diminish. It accumulates, and it tends to arrive at the worst possible moment.

We Cannot Agree

In many families, the conversation has not been avoided so much as it has been fought over and abandoned. Siblings disagree about what is needed. One person sees a crisis; another sees an overreaction. One person wants to act; another wants to wait. One person is carrying most of the caregiving weight and is exhausted; another lives far away and has a different picture of how things are. These disagreements are real and often deeply rooted. They do not resolve themselves by waiting.

We Feel Guilty

Guilt may be the most underacknowledged driver of avoidance in long-term care planning. It runs in multiple directions at once. Guilt for not having done more, sooner. Guilt for even considering a placement, for what it might say about who you are as a child, a spouse, a family. Guilt about feeling relieved that help might be coming. Guilt about your own life, your own exhaustion, the things you have had to give up. And beneath all of it, a quiet, persistent fear that choosing a care setting for someone you love means you are abandoning them.

This last fear deserves to be named directly: choosing a placement is not abandonment. It is often the opposite. It is the recognition that the person you love deserves more than you can provide alone — more consistent care, more skilled oversight, more social connection, more safety. The families who arrive at that recognition and act on it are not failing their loved ones. They are choosing them, in the fullest sense of the word. Guilt will tell you otherwise. Guilt is not always right.

What Avoidance Costs

When the conversation is deferred until a crisis forces it, several things are typically lost. The loved one's ability to participate in decisions about their own life, often the first casualty. The opportunity to plan ahead, which means fewer options, more expense, and less time to find the right placement. The chance for the transition to feel like a considered, loving choice rather than an emergency measure. And sometimes, simply the chance to say what needs to be said while there is still time to say it.

The conversation you have been avoiding is almost certainly less devastating than the one you will be forced to have if you keep avoiding it. This is not meant to alarm. It is meant to free you to begin.

How to Start: Framing and Timing

The way a conversation begins shapes everything that follows. Most hard conversations fail not because of what is said but because of how the opening lands, as an attack, an ultimatum, a confrontation, or a verdict. The person on the receiving end becomes defensive before they have heard anything, and the rest of the conversation is spent managing that defensiveness rather than actually talking.

Frame It as a Conversation, Not a Decision

The single most important framing choice is this: make clear, from the beginning, that you are not there to announce a decision. You are there to have a conversation. This is not a semantic distinction. It is the difference between a person feeling ambushed and a person feeling heard. The goal of the first conversation is not to resolve everything. It is to open the topic, share your concerns honestly, and listen. Resolution can come later. Connection comes first.

Choose the Right Moment

Timing matters more than most people realize. Do not have this conversation in the immediate aftermath of a health event, when fear and exhaustion are highest and defenses are lowest. Do not have it as an ambush during a holiday gathering, when the social stakes of the setting make honest engagement nearly impossible. Do not have it when you are angry, depleted, or running out of time. Choose a quiet moment, a planned conversation, not an improvised one, when both of you are as rested and present as the circumstances allow.

Start from Love, Not Fear

The conversation will go better if it begins from a genuine expression of love and care rather than from a list of concerns and observations. Not because the concerns are not valid — they are, but because a person who feels cared for is more able to hear hard things than a person who feels evaluated. Something as simple as: 'I want to talk about something because I love you and I've been thinking about it a lot' opens differently than 'We need to talk about what's been happening.'

What to Say — Sample Language

The following examples are not scripts. They are starting points — ways into the conversation that have worked for other families and that reflect the principles above. Adapt them to your own voice and relationship.

Opening the topic:

> *I want to talk about something that I've been carrying around for a while, and I'd rather talk about it now, when we have time to think, than wait until we don't have a choice.*

> *I've been noticing some things that worry me, not because I think something terrible is about to happen, but because I love you and I want us to have a plan before we need one.*

Inviting their perspective:

> *I'm not here to tell you what's going to happen. I want to understand how you're seeing things, what you're worried about, what matters most to you.*

> *What would feel right to you if things got harder to manage? Have you thought about what you'd want?*

Naming the hard thing:

> *I need to be honest with you about what I'm seeing,
> because I think you deserve to know what I'm thinking,
> and I want us to figure this out together rather than me
> making decisions without you.*

*These openings share something: they are honest without being
clinical, caring without being condescending, and direct without
being closed. They leave room for the other person to respond,
disagree, grieve, or simply sit with what has been said. That
room is where the conversation actually happens.*

When the Person You Love Resists

Resistance is not failure. It is almost always the first response,
and it is almost always understandable. A person who has lived
independently for decades and is now being asked to contemplate
giving that up is not being unreasonable when they push back.
They are being human. Expecting resistance, and knowing how to
respond to it — is part of being prepared.

What Resistance Usually Means

When an aging parent or spouse says 'I'm fine,' 'I don't need
help,' 'I'm not ready for that,' or 'You don't need to worry about
me' — they are not necessarily in denial about what is happening.
They may be telling you something true about their values: that
independence matters to them, that they are afraid of being a
burden, that the loss they are contemplating is terrifying, or that
they need more time. None of these are things to overcome. They
are things to hear.

Don't Try to Win the First Conversation

The impulse to resolve things — to leave the first conversation
with a plan, a decision, a next step — is understandable but often
counterproductive. If the person you love is not ready, pressing for

resolution will produce capitulation or conflict, neither of which is what you want. Plant the seed. Say what you need to say. And then let it sit. The conversation you have today changes the conversation you can have next month, even if nothing is resolved today.

Acknowledge the Loss Directly

One of the most effective things you can do in the face of resistance is to name the loss yourself — before the other person has to. 'I know this isn't what you wanted. I know how much your independence means to you. I'm not trying to take anything away from you.' When the person you love hears you acknowledge what they are afraid of losing, the conversation shifts. You are no longer adversaries. You are two people who both understand what is at stake.

When Resistance Becomes Refusal

There is a difference between a person who resists and needs time and a person who refuses in a way that is creating genuine and immediate risk. When someone's safety is at stake, when they are falling, not eating, leaving the stove on, getting lost, the conversation becomes more urgent and the family's responsibility shifts. If a loved one lacks the cognitive capacity to make safe decisions for themselves, the family may need to act even without agreement. This is painful. It is sometimes necessary. It is addressed more fully in the section on decision-making capacity below.

Talking with Someone Whose Cognition Is Changing

Conversations about care planning with someone experiencing cognitive decline require a different approach, not because the person's feelings or preferences matter less, but because the way information is processed, retained, and responded to changes with cognitive impairment. What works in a conversation with someone who is cognitively intact may not work, and can sometimes cause real distress — in a conversation with someone experiencing dementia.

Have the Conversation Earlier Than You Think You Need To

The most important guidance for families navigating cognitive decline is this: have the important conversations earlier than you think you need to. The window during which a person with early or moderate cognitive impairment can meaningfully participate in decisions about their own care — can express preferences, ask questions, understand options — is real but finite. Waiting until the decline is obvious often means waiting until the window has closed. A conversation held at what feels like 'too early' is almost always better than one held at 'too late.'

Keep It Simple and Concrete

For someone with cognitive impairment, abstract or future-oriented framing — 'What do you want to happen when you can no longer manage on your own?' — may not be processable. Concrete, present-tense framing is more likely to land. And the most effective version of that framing is the one built around what matters to this specific person.

Say the things that are relevant to your loved one. If they are social by nature, talk about the people, the activity rooms, the shared meals, the fact that there will always be someone nearby. If they have always been drawn to the outdoors, talk about the walking paths, the garden, the time outside. If they have a passion, music, cards, crafts, faith, lead with what connects to that. You are not manufacturing a sales pitch. You are speaking to what genuinely lights this person up, which is the language most likely to reach them. The goal is not to secure agreement on a care plan. It is to create a moment of real connection around something that feels true to who they are, and to do it with dignity and care, not condescension.

Focus on Feelings, Not Facts

A person with moderate to advanced dementia may not be able to process the factual content of a conversation about care planning, but they can almost always process the emotional content. Are they feeling safe? Heard? Loved? Afraid? The goal of the conversation shifts: it is less about reaching agreement on a plan and more about ensuring the person feels accompanied rather than abandoned. That is not a lesser goal. It is often the more important one.

Repeat, Revisit, and Don't Expect It to Stick

Memory impairment means that a conversation, even a meaningful and successful one — may not be retained. The person you spoke with last week may not remember the conversation this week. This is disorienting for families, but it is not a failure. The emotional residue of a warm, safe conversation often persists even when the factual content does not. You may need to have the same conversation many times. Each time is still worth having.

> *If you are navigating care planning with a loved one experiencing cognitive decline, the question to hold onto is not 'Did they understand?' It is 'Did they feel cared for?' Those are different questions, and in the middle and later stages of dementia, the second one is the one that matters most.*

When the Conversation Can No Longer Happen

There are situations in which the person at the center of a care planning conversation has lost, or never had, the capacity to participate in it meaningfully. A loved one with advanced dementia who can no longer reliably understand or communicate. A person who has suffered a stroke or traumatic brain injury that has affected their cognitive function. Someone who is medically incapacitated. In these situations, the family must make decisions on behalf of someone who cannot make them for themselves, which is among the hardest things a family is ever asked to do.

The Role of Legal Documents

If your loved one, while cognitively intact, designated a healthcare proxy or durable power of attorney for healthcare decisions, that person now steps into the decision-making role. If a healthcare directive or advance directive was created, it provides guidance about the person's wishes. These documents exist precisely for this moment. If they exist, use them. If they do not exist and your loved one still has capacity to create them, even diminished capacity — consult an elder law attorney about what is still possible.

Substituted Judgment vs. Best Interest

In the absence of clear guidance from the person themselves, families typically weigh two standards. Substituted judgment asks: what would this person have wanted, based on everything we know about them — their values, their expressed preferences, the life they lived? Best interest asks: what decision would best protect this person's wellbeing given what we know? When you can apply substituted judgment, do. It keeps the person's voice present even when they can no longer speak for themselves. When you cannot,

when you simply do not know what they would have wanted —
best interest is the standard to fall back on.

Give Yourself Permission to Grieve This Too

Making decisions for someone who cannot make them for
themselves carries its own particular weight. Families in this
situation often describe a profound sense of loneliness, the person
they would normally consult about a hard decision is the person
the decision is about. There is grief in that, and it is legitimate. You
do not have to be certain to make a good decision. You have to be
honest, thoughtful, and guided by love. That is enough.

Managing Family Disagreement

Long-term care decisions have a remarkable ability to surface
every unresolved dynamic in a family — old resentments,
competing loyalties, differences in values, inequities in caregiving
burden, and guilt that has been accumulating for years. Families
that have always functioned smoothly sometimes fracture under
the weight of these conversations. Families that have always had
tension sometimes find, in this shared difficulty, a new form of
connection. Neither outcome is guaranteed. But there are things
that help.

Name the Shared Goal

Most family disagreements about long-term care are not really
about the care decision itself. They are about competing fears,
competing guilt, and competing definitions of what it means to
love the person at the center. When the conversation gets stuck,
returning to the shared goal, the wellbeing of the person you all
love — can help. It is hard to argue about tactics when the

objective has been made explicit and everyone has agreed on it. Not impossible. But harder.

Acknowledge the Inequity

In most families, care responsibilities are not equally distributed. One person, often a daughter, often the one who lives closest — is doing the majority of the caregiving work. That person's perspective carries weight that others may not fully appreciate. If you are the sibling who lives far away and has been less present, the most valuable thing you can do in a family conversation is to acknowledge that inequity before you offer opinions about what should happen. The person who has been there deserves to be heard first.

Separate What You Know from What You Feel

Family disagreements about care often confuse two different things: what is true about the loved one's situation, and what each family member feels about it. The person who insists 'Dad is fine' may be reporting on a recent good visit, which is true — while the primary caregiver is reporting on a pattern of decline that a single visit does not capture. Separating observations from feelings, and being honest about which is which, can help the conversation move from argument to information-sharing.

When Families Cannot Agree

Sometimes families cannot reach agreement, and the situation requires action anyway. If safety is at stake, the primary caregiver or designated healthcare proxy may need to make a decision even without consensus. If legal authority is unclear or contested, an elder law attorney can help clarify who has decision-making standing. If the conflict is serious and sustained, a professional mediator or family therapist experienced in eldercare transitions can sometimes help families find a path forward when they cannot find one on their own.

What to Do When a Sibling Is Obstructing

A specific and painful situation: a sibling who is actively blocking necessary care, either through denial, through emotional pressure on the loved one to refuse help, or through refusal to participate in care planning. This happens, and it is more common than families who have not faced it realize. If this is your situation, document your concerns and communications in writing. Consult an elder law attorney about the legal framework for decision-making in your state. And if the obstruction is creating genuine risk for your loved one, know that the courts can and do intervene in situations where a family cannot agree and someone's safety is at stake.

After the Conversation

Having the conversation is not the end. It is the beginning of an ongoing process — of checking in, of updating the plan as circumstances change, of returning to hard topics when they resurface. A few things worth keeping in mind as you move forward.

Write down what was said and agreed to. Memory is imperfect, especially under emotional stress. A brief written summary of a care conversation, even just notes to yourself — can be invaluable when the same conversation needs to happen again with a sibling who was not present, or with a care team, or with an admissions coordinator.

Follow up. A conversation that ends with 'let's think about it' is not a closed loop. Set a time to return to the topic, not as a deadline or an ultimatum, but as a genuine continuation. 'Can we talk again in a few weeks?' honors both the need for more time and the need to keep moving.

Involve the right people at the right time. A physician, a social worker, a geriatric care manager, or a family therapist can sometimes say things in a professional capacity that a son or daughter cannot say in a personal one. If the conversation keeps stalling, consider whether bringing in a trusted outside voice might help it move.

Be patient with yourself. These conversations are hard because the situation is hard, not because you are doing them wrong. If the first one does not go well, it still moves something. If the person you love is angry or withdrawn afterward, give it time. The conversation plants something even when it does not immediately resolve anything.

> *You do not have to do this perfectly. You have to do it honestly, and with love, and keep doing it even when it is hard. That is all that is ever required.*

When the Conversation Doesn't Resolve — And Action Is Still Required

Most of this chapter has been about what to do when a conversation is hard but still possible, when the person you love resists but is present, when the family disagrees but is still engaging, when the path forward is unclear but there is still time to find it. But there is a harder situation that deserves a direct answer: what happens when someone flat-out refuses, or when family disagreement cannot be resolved, and action is still necessary?

When Your Loved One Refuses

A loved one who is cognitively intact has the legal right to make decisions about their own life, including the decision to refuse help, to remain at home against your better judgment, or to decline a placement you believe is necessary. This is painful, and it is real. As long as a person has decision-making capacity, their autonomy must be respected even when their choices frighten you.

What you can do: continue the conversation. Not as pressure, but as presence. Stay involved, stay connected, and keep the door open. Document your concerns in writing — to yourself, to a physician, to an elder law attorney — so there is a record of what you observed and when. This is not ammunition to get what you want. It is evidence you care and are concerned. Ask the person's physician to weigh in; sometimes a trusted doctor can say things a family member cannot. And if the situation deteriorates to the point where safety is at real risk and the person's capacity to make safe decisions is in question, consult an elder law attorney about what legal options exist in your state — including, in extreme cases, guardianship.

What you cannot do: make the decision for a person who has capacity and is refusing. This is one of the hardest truths in elder care. Sometimes the most loving thing you can do is stay present, stay honest, and wait for the person to be ready, or for the circumstances to change in a way that makes the conversation possible again.

When the Family Cannot Agree and Time Is Running Out

When a family is genuinely deadlocked and the situation requires action, the path forward usually runs through clarity about who has legal decision-making authority. If a healthcare proxy or durable power of attorney exists, that person has the authority to make the decision, and should. If it does not exist and the loved one still has capacity, the priority is to get those documents created immediately, while there is still time. If the loved one no longer has capacity and no documents exist, an elder law attorney can help the family understand the legal framework for who has decision-making standing under state law.

If a family member is actively obstructing a necessary decision, not just disagreeing, but blocking action in a way that is creating genuine risk — know that the legal system has mechanisms for exactly this situation. Courts can and do appoint guardians when families cannot agree and someone's safety requires a decision. This is a path of last resort, and it is a difficult one. But it exists, and it is sometimes the right one.

> *If you are in a situation where the conversation has failed and action is still required, you are not out of options. You may need professional help, a physician, a social worker, an elder law attorney, or a mediator — to move forward. Asking for that help is not giving up. It is doing what the situation requires.*

Key Takeaways from Chapter Seven

Avoidance is not protection. The conversation deferred until a crisis arrives is almost always harder than the one held earlier, and costs the loved one the ability to participate in their own future.

Guilt is one of the most powerful drivers of avoidance. Choosing a care placement is not abandonment. It is often the most loving decision a family can make, and guilt, while understandable, is not a reliable guide.

Frame it as a conversation, not a decision. The goal of the first conversation is to open the topic and listen, not to resolve everything. Resolution follows connection.

Resistance is almost always understandable and almost never the final word. Acknowledge the loss the person is contemplating. Don't press for agreement before they are ready.

Conversations with someone experiencing cognitive decline require earlier timing, simpler framing, and a shift in goal: from reaching agreement on a plan to ensuring the person feels accompanied rather than abandoned.

When a loved one has lost decision-making capacity, use legal documents if they exist, apply substituted judgment when possible, and give yourself permission to grieve the weight of making decisions for someone who cannot make them for themselves.

Family disagreements are normal and often run deeper than the immediate care question. Naming the shared goal, acknowledging inequities in caregiving burden, and separating observations from feelings can help families find a way forward.

If the conversation fails and action is still required, clarity about legal decision-making authority is the starting point. An elder law attorney, a trusted physician, or a professional mediator can help move things forward when the family cannot. You are not out of options.

ACTION STEP:

> *Identify the conversation you have been avoiding. Name it specifically: is it the conversation with your loved one about what is changing? The one with your siblings about what needs to happen? The one with a parent about their wishes while they can still express them? Choose one conversation, not all of them, just one, and decide when you will have it.*

Not 'sometime soon.' A specific time. Then use this chapter to prepare for it.

You have had the conversation. Chapter Eight, Making the Decision, addresses what comes next: how to weigh everything you have learned, how to know when the time is actually right, how to involve your loved one in the final decision where possible, and how to move forward with clarity and confidence when the moment arrives.

CHAPTER EIGHT

Making the Decision

Here is what no one tells you about the moment you finally make this decision: it may not feel the way you expected it to.

Families who have been circling this choice for months, sometimes years, often imagine that when the moment comes, it will arrive with clarity. That something will happen, or enough things will accumulate, and the path forward will become obvious. What they find instead is that the moment may arrive quietly, and with ambivalence still attached. They make the decision and still wonder if they are doing the right thing. They feel grief and relief simultaneously, sometimes within the same breath. They move forward not because all doubt has been resolved — it rarely is, but because waiting has become more costly than acting.

This is normal. This is, in fact, what making a good decision under genuine uncertainty looks like. The families who wait for certainty before acting often wait too long. The families who act before they feel ready, who trust what they have learned, honor what they know, and move forward with love even when doubt is still present — these families tend to look back and recognize that they got it right, even if it never felt that way in the moment.

This chapter is about making that decision — how to know when the time is actually right, what to do when you are still not sure, how to involve your loved one where possible, what the moment of commitment feels like and how to move through it, and what happens in the days immediately after. It is the chapter that brings together everything this book has been building toward.

> *You may not feel ready. Readiness, in the way most families imagine it, that calm, certain, unambiguous knowing — is not how this works. What you will have, if you have done the work this book describes, is something better: enough information, enough clarity, and enough love to act. That is what readiness actually looks like.*

How to Know When the Time Is Actually Right

The question families ask most often, and most urgently — is: how do I know when it's time? They want a threshold, a number, a specific set of criteria that, when met, will give them permission to act. The honest answer is that there is no single threshold, and there never will be. But there are patterns — reliable clusters of signals that, taken together, consistently indicate that the time has come or is approaching.

The Accumulation Pattern

In most situations, the decision does not hinge on a single dramatic event. It hinges on accumulation — on the weight of many smaller things that have been building over time. A person who has fallen twice, who is no longer managing medications reliably, whose home has begun to show signs of neglect, and whose primary caregiver is running on empty is in a different situation from a person who has had one fall and is otherwise managing well. The accumulation pattern — multiple signals present simultaneously, each manageable in isolation but telling in combination — is the most common and reliable indicator that a transition is needed.

Look at your When Readiness Checklist. If you have been completing it as you have moved through this book, you now have a documented picture of where things stand across safety, function, cognition, finances, and facility research. If signals are present across multiple domains, not just one, that is meaningful. The Checklist is not a decision algorithm. But it is a mirror, and sometimes the mirror shows you something you have been working hard not to see.

When a Crisis Has Already Happened

Sometimes the decision is not made before the crisis — it is made in the middle of one. A hospitalization, a fall with injury, a sudden and significant cognitive decline. If this is where you find yourself, the decision about timing has in some sense already been made for you. What remains is the decision about where, which facility, which level of care, which placement serves your loved one best given what you now know. The tools in this book still apply. The evaluation framework from Chapter Six still applies. You are working faster and under more pressure, but you are not working without guidance.

The Caregiver Signal

One indicator that families frequently underweight is the state of the primary caregiver. When the person doing the caregiving has reached the point of genuine depletion, when their own health is being affected, when fear has become a constant companion, when they can no longer provide the level of care the situation requires, that is a signal about the loved one's needs as much as it is a signal about the caregiver's limits. A care arrangement that is destroying the caregiver is not, by definition, a sustainable care arrangement. The loved one deserves better than that. And so does the caregiver.

What 'Right' Looks Like

The time is right when the signals are clear enough, the research is sufficient, and the available options are better than the current situation. It does not require that every question be answered, that every family member be in agreement, or that the person you love has accepted what is coming. It requires that the weight of what you know points clearly in one direction, and that waiting will not make the situation better, only harder.

What to Do When You're Still Not Sure

Uncertainty at this stage is not a sign that you have not done enough work. It is almost always a sign that you are taking the decision seriously. The families who feel no uncertainty at this stage are often the ones who have been through a prolonged crisis and have arrived at a point of exhaustion that looks like clarity. The families still sitting with genuine doubt are often the ones who have options, which means they have done something right.

Name What You Are Uncertain About

Uncertainty is easier to work with when it is specific. 'I'm not sure' is not a workable state. 'I'm not sure whether the memory care unit at this facility is the right fit, given what I observed on the tour' is a workable state, because it points toward a specific question that can be investigated further, or a specific concern that can be raised directly with the facility. Take the time to name what, precisely, you are uncertain about. Write it down. Then ask whether more information would resolve it, or whether it is uncertainty that no amount of information will eliminate.

Distinguish Informational Uncertainty from Emotional Uncertainty

There are two kinds of uncertainty at this stage, and they require different responses. Informational uncertainty means there are things you still need to know, a question about a facility's Medicaid policy, a tour you have not yet completed, a financial figure that needs to be confirmed. That kind of uncertainty has a remedy: get the information. Emotional uncertainty is different. It is the grief, the guilt, the fear that no additional fact will resolve, because it is not really a question about information. It is a question about love, and loss, and the hardness of what you are doing. That kind of uncertainty does not need to be resolved before you act. It needs to be acknowledged, carried, and moved through.

Get a Second Opinion

If you have done thorough research and still feel stuck, consider whether an outside perspective would help. A geriatric care manager, a professional whose entire job is assessing care needs and evaluating options — can review the situation and offer a professional judgment about timing and placement that is not filtered through the love and grief that makes your own judgment harder. A trusted physician who knows your loved one well can weigh in on the clinical picture. And do not underestimate the value of a friend or colleague who has personally been through this process — someone who has sat where you are sitting and come out the other side can offer a perspective that no professional can fully replicate. These are not signs that you cannot make this decision. They are signs that you are taking it seriously enough to want the best available information.

Trust the Pattern More Than the Moment

Cognitive impairment, functional decline, and caregiver exhaustion all fluctuate day to day. Your loved one will have good days and bad days. The caregiver will have moments of genuine capability and moments of depletion. Decisions made on good days tend toward delay; decisions made on bad days tend toward panic. Neither is reliable. What is reliable is the pattern, the documented trend over weeks and months that shows you where things are actually going, independent of today's particular circumstances. Trust the pattern. It is more honest than the moment.

> *Waiting for certainty is a reasonable impulse and an unreliable strategy. The question to ask is not 'Am I certain?' It is 'Do I know enough, and is waiting to make this decision better or worse?' If the honest answer to the second question is 'worse,' you have your answer.*

Involving Your Loved One in the Final Decision

Where it is possible to involve the person most affected in the final decision, it should be done. Not as a formality, not as a performance of consultation that has already been decided, but as a genuine act of respect for the person whose life this decision will shape. The degree to which this is possible will depend on cognitive capacity, emotional readiness, and how the conversations leading up to this moment have gone. But the principle holds: their voice belongs in this decision wherever it can be.

What Involvement Can Look Like

Involvement does not always mean agreement or co-authorship of the decision. For someone with intact cognitive capacity, it can mean a genuine conversation about the options, their preferences among facilities, what they most want their daily life to include, and what they are most afraid of. For someone with moderate cognitive impairment, it might mean a tour of the facility where they can form impressions and express how they feel, even if they cannot fully process the decision itself. For someone with advanced dementia, involvement might be as simple as ensuring that what you know about who they are — their history, their preferences, the things that have always brought them comfort — is built into the placement decision. Their voice can be present even when they can no longer speak for themselves.

When They Do Not Want to Be Involved

Some people, when it becomes clear that a transition is coming, make a deliberate choice to step back from the decision — to say, in effect, 'I trust you. You decide.' This is not passivity or defeat. For some people, it is the most dignified way they know to face something they cannot change. Honor it. Do not press for engagement that the person has indicated they do not want. Make the best decision you can, keep them informed at whatever level feels right to them, and let them know — clearly and often, that they are loved and that this decision comes from that love.

When They Disagree with the Decision

A loved one who disagrees with the decision but lacks the capacity to safely make their own care choices presents one of the most painful situations in elder care. There is no way to make this easy. What you can do is be honest with them about what is happening and why, avoid deceiving them about where they are going or what will happen there, and stay as present as possible through the transition itself. Presence — visiting frequently, calling regularly, advocating actively for their care — is the most powerful statement you can make that this decision was made with love and not as abandonment.

The Moment of Commitment

There is a specific moment in this process, when the deposit is made, when the admission paperwork is signed, when the date is set, that is different in kind from everything that came before it. Up until that moment, the decision has existed in a space of possibility. After that, the decision is real. Most families find this moment harder than they expected, even when they were fully prepared for it.

What You May Feel

Grief. Relief. Guilt. Exhaustion. A strange flatness where you expected something more clarifying. The feeling that you should be more certain than you are, or more at peace than you are, or less sad than you are. All of these are normal. None of them mean you have made the wrong decision. They mean you are a person who loves someone and has just done one of the hardest things a person is asked to do. Give yourself permission to feel all of it.

Second-Guessing

Almost every family second-guesses this decision at least once, and most second-guess it many times — particularly in the early weeks after the transition, when the adjustment is hardest and everything feels uncertain. This is not a signal that you were wrong. It is a signal that you care. The question to hold onto in those moments is not 'Did I make the right choice?', which cannot be answered with certainty in either direction. It is: 'Did I make a thoughtful, informed, loving choice with what I knew at the time?' If the answer to that question is yes, you made the right decision. The rest is adjustment, not error.

The Transition Is Not the Decision

One important distinction: the difficulty of the transition period, the adjustment, the grief, the disruption that follows any major life change — is not evidence that the decision was wrong. Transitions are hard even when the underlying decision was right. A loved one who struggles in the first weeks of a new placement is not proving that the placement was a mistake. They are going through what most people go through when their world has changed. Most adjust. Most find their footing. The research on long-term care transitions consistently shows that the initial adjustment period, however hard, does not predict the longer-term outcome.

> *The decision and the transition are two different things. Judge the decision by the quality of the process that produced it, the information gathered, the conversations had, the care taken. Do not judge it by the difficulty of the weeks that follow. Transitions are hard. That is not the same as wrong.*

What Happens Immediately After the Decision

Once the decision is made and a placement is confirmed, there is a practical dimension that requires attention. The emotional weight of this moment can make it hard to shift into logistics, but the logistics matter, and managing them well makes the transition itself go better.

Before the Move-In Date

The period between the decision and the actual move is when the groundwork for a good transition is laid. Several things are worth attending to in this window:

Communicate with the facility's care team. Share everything you know about your loved one — their history, their preferences, their routines, what comforts them and what agitates them, the names they go by, the things that matter most to them. The care team will have an intake process, but your knowledge of this person goes deeper than any intake form. Use it.

Prepare the room. Personal items — photographs, a familiar blanket, objects that carry meaning — make a new space feel less foreign. Familiar sensory cues matter, particularly for people with cognitive impairment. Take the time to make the space feel like theirs before they arrive.

Notify the right people. Physicians, specialists, pharmacies, and insurance carriers all need to know about the transition. Coordinate the transfer of medical records and medication lists. Ensure that the receiving facility has a complete and current picture of the medical situation before the first day.

Plan the move-in day carefully. Who will be there, how the arrival will be framed, what will happen in the first hours. The first day sets a tone. A calm, warm, well-prepared arrival, with familiar faces present, a room that already feels personal, and staff who have been briefed — is a meaningfully better start than an improvised one.

The First Weeks

The first two to four weeks after a care transition are typically the hardest, for the resident, for the family, and sometimes for the care team. A few things that help:

Visit frequently, but not so frequently that you disrupt the adjustment process. There is a balance here that varies by person. Some residents settle better with a gradual reduction in family presence; others need more contact early on. Talk to the care team about what they are observing and adjust accordingly.

Raise concerns early and through the right channels. If something is not right, a medication error, a care gap, a dignity concern — address it promptly and directly with the appropriate staff member. You are your loved one's advocate. That role does not end at move-in.

Ask whether the facility has a Family Portal. Many communities now offer secure digital portals that give family members access to high-level information about their loved one — activity participation, care notes, updates from the team. If one is available, get access to it early and share it with other family members who want to stay informed. It is one of the most practical tools available for staying connected to your loved one's daily life without requiring a phone call every time you have a question.

Give the adjustment time before drawing conclusions. The first week is almost always the hardest. The second week is usually somewhat better. By the end of the first month, most residents have begun to establish routines and connections, and the picture of how the placement is actually going becomes clearer. Do not make permanent judgments based on temporary adjustment pain.

Take care of yourself. The period immediately after a care transition is often when family members, particularly primary caregivers, finally crash. The adrenaline of the decision and the move is gone, and what remains is grief, exhaustion, and sometimes a disorienting absence of the caregiving role that has organized so much of their life. This is normal. It is also a signal that rest and support are needed. You cannot sustain the advocacy your loved one needs if you have nothing left.

Ongoing: You Are Still Their Family

A placement is not an ending. It is a transition, from one form of care to another, from one living situation to another. Your role in your loved one's life does not end at move-in. It changes. You are no longer the primary caregiver managing day-to-day logistics. You are the person who knows them best, who advocates for them, who visits and calls and notices things that the staff, however skilled and caring, cannot notice the way you can. That role matters. The research on long-term care outcomes consistently shows that residents with engaged, present families receive better care. Your presence is not just comfort. It is protection.

> *Making this decision was not the end of loving your loved one. It was an act of it. Stay present. Stay engaged. Keep showing up. That is what love looks like from here.*

Key Takeaways from Chapter Eight

You may not feel ready. Readiness is not the absence of doubt — it is having enough information, enough clarity, and enough love to act in spite of it.

The time is right when signals are present across multiple domains, when waiting is making the situation worse rather than better, and when the available options are better than the current situation. There is no single threshold.

Distinguish informational uncertainty, which has a remedy, from emotional uncertainty, which must be acknowledged and carried, not resolved before acting.

Trust the pattern over the moment. Good days and bad days are not reliable guides. The documented trend over weeks and months is.

Involve your loved one in the final decision wherever possible, not as a formality, but as a genuine act of respect. Their voice belongs in this decision at whatever level their capacity allows.

The moment of commitment will be harder than you expect, and the feelings that come with it, grief, relief, guilt, ambivalence, are normal. They are not evidence that you chose wrong.

Second-guessing is almost universal. Judge the decision by the quality of the process that produced it, not by the difficulty of the weeks that follow. Transitions are hard. That is not the same as wrong.

Your role does not end at move-in. Residents with engaged, present families receive better care. Stay present, stay engaged, and keep advocating. That is what love looks like from here.

ACTION STEP:

Pull out your When Readiness Checklist. Look at it with fresh eyes, not as a list of things still undone, but as a picture of where you actually stand. If signals are present across multiple sections, ask yourself honestly: is there a decision being deferred here that shouldn't be? If the answer is yes, name the specific thing that is holding you back. Then use this chapter to determine whether that thing is an information gap, which can be closed, or an emotional weight that needs to be carried forward rather than resolved.

The decision has been made. Chapter Nine, The Transition, goes deeper into what the move itself looks like — how to prepare your loved one, how to manage move-in day, how to get through the adjustment period, and how to build a relationship with the care team that serves your loved one well for the long term.

CHAPTER NINE

The Transition

The decision is made. The placement is confirmed. And now something shifts, from the long, exhausting work of planning toward something more immediate and more tender: the actual movement of a person from the life they have known into something new. This is the transition. And it is its own chapter in the story of this family, with its own demands, its own grace notes, and its own particular kind of hard.

In my experience, the transition period is where the emotional weight of this whole process tends to land. The planning phase has the structure of a problem to be solved — there are checklists, research, conversations, decisions. The transition has none of that protective scaffolding. It is just the reality of what is happening: a person you love is moving into a care setting, and everything that means is present all at once. The grief. The relief. The strangeness. The love.

What I want families to know is this: the transition period is finite. It has a shape. The first days are the hardest. The first two weeks are hard in a different way. By the end of the first month, most residents have begun to find their footing, a familiar face on the nursing staff, a routine that is starting to feel like their own, a meal they look forward to. It does not always happen on that timeline. But it happens far more often than families in the thick of the first week are able to believe. The transition is not the destination. It is the passage.

> *The goal of everything in this chapter is not to make the transition painless — it will not be. It is to make it as good as it can be: prepared, loving, well-supported, and followed by the kind of ongoing presence that helps a person find their way in a new place.*

Preparing Your Loved One Emotionally for the Move

The period between the decision and the move is not empty waiting time. It is an opportunity — to help the person you love begin to orient toward what is coming, at whatever level their capacity allows. How you use this window will depend significantly on where they are cognitively and emotionally, but the underlying principle is the same regardless: the more familiar something feels before it happens, the less frightening it is when it does.

For Someone Who Is Cognitively Intact

If your loved one is cognitively intact and aware of the transition, this period calls for honest, ongoing conversation. Not a single difficult talk followed by silence, but a series of smaller conversations — about what the facility is like, what their room will look like, what a typical day might involve, what they are most looking forward to and most anxious about. Let them ask questions. If you do not know the answer, find out. Visit the facility together more than once if possible — familiarity with the physical space reduces the shock of arrival. Involve them in preparing their room: which photographs, which chair, which objects from home will come with them. These decisions are small in the practical sense. They are not small in the psychological sense.

For Someone with Cognitive Impairment

For a person with dementia or significant cognitive impairment, detailed advance preparation of the kind described above may not be possible, and attempting it may cause more distress than it prevents. The guidance from Chapter Seven applies here: keep it simple, keep it concrete, and focus on feelings rather than facts. You do not need to explain everything. You need to ensure that the person feels safe and loved in the days leading up to the move, and that the move itself is handled with as much warmth and calm as you can bring to it.

One practical note: for people with dementia, the day of the move is often less distressing than the family anticipates, particularly if the environment is warm and welcoming and familiar faces are present. It is sometimes the family members who struggle most on move-in day, and that is worth knowing in advance, so it does not catch you off guard.

What to Tell Them About What Is Happening

Honesty is almost always the right policy, adapted to the person's capacity to receive it. For someone who is cognitively intact, be clear about what is happening and why. Avoid softening the truth to the point of misleading them — people generally sense when they are not being told the full story, and discovering that later damages trust. For someone with cognitive impairment, the framing matters more than the detail: this is a safe place, people here will take good care of you, I will be here with you and I will come back. Those statements are true, and they are the ones that matter most. For a deeper guide to adjusting how you communicate with someone experiencing cognitive decline, including how to avoid language and framing that can cause unnecessary distress — return to Chapter Seven, which covers this in detail.

Move-In Day: What to Do, What to Expect, How to Help

Move-in day is one of the most important days in this entire process, for the person moving, for the family accompanying them, and in some ways for the relationship between the family and the facility. How it goes sets a tone that echoes forward. Preparing for it carefully is worth the effort.

Before You Arrive

The room should be ready before your loved one walks through the door. If the facility allows early access, and many do — use it. Bring the personal items in advance: the photographs arranged on the dresser, the familiar blanket on the bed, the chair positioned where they like to sit. The goal is that when they arrive, the room already has something of them in it. It is not their home. But it should feel like it could become one.

Brief the care team the morning of the move, or the day before. Share anything that will help staff make a good first impression: the name they go by, a subject they love to talk about, something that comforts them when they are anxious, something that agitates them when it goes wrong. The intake paperwork captures the clinical facts. This conversation captures the person.

Who Should Be There

Bring the people who matter most, but keep the group small. A move-in that involves the whole family — multiple siblings, grandchildren, cousins — can feel overwhelming and circus-like rather than warm and grounding. Two or three people who know and love the person well, who can stay calm and present through whatever the day brings, is usually the right number. This is not a celebration. It is a passage, and it deserves the intimacy that passages require.

How to Frame the Day

How you talk about the day, to your loved one and to yourself, matters. Avoid framing it as a goodbye or an ending, even internally, because that framing leaks into your affect and your loved one will feel it. Frame it instead as an arrival: this is where you live now, let's get you settled, let me show you around. If there is something about the facility your loved one has expressed genuine interest in, a garden, a music program, a particular staff member they connected with on a tour — lead with that. Arrival into something, not departure from something.

When to Leave

Knowing when to leave on move-in day is one of the harder judgment calls families face. Staying too long can delay the person's adjustment and make separation harder when it finally comes. Leaving too abruptly can feel like abandonment. A good general principle: stay until your loved one is settled — until they have eaten something, met a few staff members, and seem oriented to the space, and then say a warm, clear goodbye. Not 'I'll be right back' if you will not be. Not an open-ended hover that makes leaving harder for everyone. A clear, loving goodbye, with a specific time you will return: 'I'll be back tomorrow at two.' That specificity is grounding for both of you.

> *The hardest moment on move-in day is often the one in the parking lot, after you have said goodbye and walked out. Give yourself space for that. It is the right response to something genuinely hard. It does not mean you made the wrong decision. It means you love this person, and you just did something very difficult on their behalf.*

The Adjustment Period: What's Normal and What's Not

The adjustment period — roughly the first four to six weeks after move-in — is the phase that most families find hardest to manage emotionally. Your loved one may be sad, confused, angry, or withdrawn. They may ask repeatedly to go home. They may seem worse than they did before the move. Families watching this often conclude that the placement was a mistake. In most cases, they are wrong. What they are seeing is adjustment, and adjustment, however painful to witness, is not the same as deterioration.

What Is Normal

In the first days and weeks after a move, it is normal to see:

Sadness, tearfulness, or expressions of wanting to go home — particularly in the first week, and often most intense in the evenings.

Confusion or disorientation, especially in people with cognitive impairment — new environments are harder to adjust to than familiar ones, and this often improves a great deal as the person builds familiarity with the space and the staff.

Withdrawal or reduced social engagement — it takes time to feel comfortable enough to participate in a new community, and introverted or anxious individuals may take longer than others.

Changes in sleep, appetite, or behavior — these are common responses to environmental change and usually stabilize within the first month.

Anger directed at family members, sometimes the person who feels safest to be angry at is the one who loves you most. This is painful but usually temporary.

The general arc of adjustment — harder in week one, somewhat better in week two, meaningfully improved by the end of week four — holds for most residents in most settings. It does not hold for everyone, and it does not mean the early weeks are not real or do not matter. But knowing the arc exists can help families hold on through the hardest part without drawing permanent conclusions too soon.

What Is Not Normal, and Warrants Attention

Adjustment pain is expected. There are signals, however, that go beyond normal adjustment and warrant prompt attention, either with the care team or, if the response is inadequate, with facility administration:

Rapid or significant physical decline — unexplained weight loss, new injuries, worsening of medical conditions that were previously stable.

Signs of neglect — consistent evidence that basic care needs (hygiene, meals, medication) are not being met.

Expressions of fear related to specific staff members or specific situations, not general anxiety, but specific, repeated statements or behavioral signals that something is wrong.

Isolation that is facility-driven rather than resident-chosen, a person who is being kept in their room, excluded from activities, or not being encouraged to engage.

Staff who are consistently dismissive, disrespectful, or unable to answer basic questions about your loved one's care.

Trust your instincts. You know this person. If something feels wrong beyond the expected texture of adjustment, do not wait and hope it resolves. Raise it. The section on advocacy below describes how to do that effectively.

Building a Relationship with the Care Team

The quality of your loved one's daily life in a care setting is shaped, more than any other single factor, by the people who provide their care. The nurses, aides, therapists, and activity staff who interact with your loved one every day are not interchangeable service providers. They are the people who will know whether your loved one had a good night, who will notice when something seems off, who will choose — in the dozens of small moments that do not show up on any care plan, whether to linger or move on. Your relationship with them matters enormously.

How to Show Up as a Partner, Not an Adversary

Families who approach the care team as adversaries to be monitored tend to get a certain kind of response: defensive, careful, guarded. Families who approach the care team as partners in caring for someone they both love tend to get a different kind: open, communicative, engaged. Both families may be equally vigilant about their loved one's care. The one who has built a relationship will almost always get better information and better access.

This does not mean ignoring problems or softening legitimate concerns. It means leading with appreciation when appreciation is warranted, learning the names of the people who care for your loved one daily, asking how they are doing and meaning it, sharing what you know about your loved one that helps them do their job better. The aide who knows that your mother was a schoolteacher who loves crossword puzzles will interact with her differently than the aide who sees a name on a chart. You are the person who can make that introduction.

Showing Appreciation, and What That Can Look Like

Care work is demanding, often underrecognized, and done by people who have chosen to show up every day for some of the most vulnerable members of our communities. When you encounter staff who are doing their jobs with skill and genuine warmth, saying so matters, and there are more ways to do it than most families realize.

Write it down. A note to the Nursing Home Administrator or Director of Nursing recognizing a specific staff member by name, describing what they did and why it mattered, carries real weight. These letters often go into personnel files and matter for careers. Take five minutes and write one.

Say it publicly. Online reviews, facility survey responses, and social media posts that name and thank specific staff members are meaningful and visible in ways a private conversation is not. If a facility has a comment card or satisfaction survey, complete it, and be specific about what was done well.

Small gestures. Baked goods, a card, a simple expression of gratitude go a long way in settings where staff often work long shifts with little recognition. Note that some facilities have policies limiting what staff can accept, if you are unsure, ask. The intent matters even when the gesture needs to be adjusted.

Show up as a volunteer. If you have time and the facility welcomes family participation, letting the activities team know you are available — to help with a program, to read to residents, to simply be present — deepens your connection to the community and signals that you see the staff as collaborators.

Respect their expertise. There is a meaningful difference between raising a legitimate concern and telling someone how to do their job. Staff are professionals who are caring for many residents, not just yours. Trust your instincts about when something needs to be said, and how to say it in a way that invites collaboration rather than closes it down. Their primary responsibility is to the residents in their care. Honor that.

Who to Know and How to Reach Them

In any care setting, there are a handful of people whose roles make them particularly important to know by name and to have a direct line to:

The charge nurse or unit nurse, the clinical lead on your loved one's floor or unit, the person to call first when a medical or care concern arises.

The primary aide, certified nursing assistant (CNA), or care partner, the direct care staff member who provides most of your loved one's daily personal care. This person often knows your loved one better than anyone in the building.

The social worker or care coordinator, the person who manages care planning, family communication, and transitions. Your primary contact for non-clinical questions and concerns.

The director of nursing, the clinical leader of the facility. Not the first call for routine concerns, but important to know for situations that are not being resolved at the floor level.

The activities director or recreational therapist — particularly important for residents whose quality of life is largely shaped by programming and social engagement.

The Care Plan Meeting

Most care settings hold formal care plan meetings at regular intervals — typically within the first two weeks of admission and then quarterly, or whenever there is a significant change in condition. These meetings bring together the clinical, social, and therapeutic team to review the resident's status, update the care plan, and hear from the family. Attend these meetings. Prepare for them. Bring your observations, your questions, and your knowledge of who this person is and what matters to them. The care plan is the document that governs your loved one's daily care — you have both the right and the responsibility to participate in shaping it.

Staying Connected Between Visits

Beyond in-person visits, ask about the tools the facility provides for staying connected: family portals, communication logs, scheduled calls with the care team. Establish a rhythm that works for your family, who calls when, who attends which meetings, how information gets shared among siblings or other family members who cannot always be present. A family that is organized and consistent in its engagement is easier for the care team to work with, and more effective as advocates for the person they love.

When Something Goes Wrong: How to Advocate Effectively

Even in excellent facilities, things go wrong. Medications get missed. Care needs are underestimated. A staff member has an off day in a way that affects your loved one. A concern you raised last week has not been addressed. How you handle these moments — how you advocate for your loved one when something is not right — is one of the most important skills you will use in this phase.

Start at the Right Level

Most concerns should be raised first with the person closest to the issue, the floor nurse, the primary aide, the social worker. Escalating immediately to administration for every concern exhausts goodwill and makes it harder to get traction on the issues that actually require higher-level attention. Start at the floor level. Be specific about what you observed or were told, when it happened, and what you are asking for. Give a reasonable timeframe for a response. Document the conversation in writing, a brief follow-up email that says 'Following up on our conversation today about X' creates a record without being adversarial.

When to Escalate

Escalate when a concern at the floor level has not been resolved within a reasonable timeframe, when the issue involves a pattern rather than an isolated incident, or when the safety or dignity of your loved one is at immediate risk. The escalation path in most facilities runs from floor staff to charge nurse to director of nursing to administrator. In situations involving potential abuse, neglect, or serious safety violations, you also have the right, and sometimes the obligation — to contact your state's long-term care ombudsman, an independent advocate whose job is to investigate complaints and protect residents' rights.

How to Advocate Without Burning Bridges

Effective advocacy is specific, documented, persistent, and focused on the outcome rather than the grievance. 'My mother has been in the same clothes for two days and her call light went unanswered for forty minutes yesterday. I need to understand what happened and what will change' is effective advocacy. 'Nobody here cares about her and this place is terrible' is not, not because the feeling is wrong, but because it closes the conversation rather than opening it.

Stay focused on what you want changed and by when. Put things in writing when they are serious. Follow up when commitments are made and not kept. Know your rights — residents in licensed care facilities have legally protected rights, and every facility is required to post them. And if you find yourself consistently unable to resolve concerns through normal channels, bring in outside help: the ombudsman, an elder law attorney, or a geriatric care manager who can advocate alongside you.

> *Your presence — consistent, engaged, and known to the staff — is itself a form of protection. Residents whose families visit regularly and ask questions receive closer attention. This is not a cynical observation. It is simply how human systems work. Show up. Be known. Keep asking.*

Knowing When a Placement Isn't Working

Most placements, given adequate time and engaged family advocacy, do work. Most adjustment periods resolve into something more settled. But not always, and families need to know how to distinguish between a placement that is working its way through a hard transition and one that is not the right fit, or where the quality of care is not acceptable.

The Difference Between Adjustment and a Bad Fit

Adjustment looks like: sadness that is gradually diminishing, confusion that is slowly resolving as the environment becomes familiar, resistance that softens over weeks as relationships with staff develop. A bad fit or poor quality care looks like: problems that are not resolving despite time and advocacy, a pattern of concerns that recurs after each apparent resolution, a loved one whose physical condition or emotional state is declining rather than stabilizing, or a care team that is consistently unresponsive to reasonable concerns.

How Long to Give It

The general guidance is to give a placement at least four to six weeks before drawing firm conclusions — long enough for the initial adjustment period to run its course. This does not mean ignoring serious concerns for six weeks. It means not making permanent decisions about a placement based on the first week's experience. If concerns are present and serious, raise them. Give the facility the opportunity to respond and correct. If the response is inadequate or the problems recur, that is meaningful information about whether this placement can be made to work.

Deciding to Move

The decision to move a loved one from one placement to another is not one to make lightly — moves are disruptive, particularly for people with cognitive impairment, and the adjustment process starts over with each one. But staying in a placement that is not working, where care quality is consistently poor, where concerns are not being addressed, or where the level of care simply does not match the person's needs — is also a decision with consequences. The evaluation framework from Chapter Six still applies. The same questions that guided the original placement decision guide this one. You have done this before. You can do it again.

> *A placement that is not working is not evidence that you chose wrong — it is evidence that circumstances have changed, or that what was adequate before is no longer adequate now, or that the facility has not held up its end of the relationship. Recognizing that and acting on it is not failure. It is the same loving advocacy that brought you here in the first place.*

Key Takeaways from Chapter Nine

The transition period has a shape. The first days are the hardest. Most residents find their footing within the first month. The transition is the passage, not the destination.

Preparation in the weeks before move-in matters. Use that window to orient your loved one, involve them in preparing their space, and brief the care team on who this person is beyond their diagnosis.

Move-in day sets a tone. Keep the group small, prepare the room in advance, frame it as an arrival rather than a departure, and say a clear, loving goodbye with a specific return time rather than an open-ended hover.

Adjustment pain is normal. Sadness, confusion, withdrawal, and anger in the first weeks are expected responses to major change, not evidence that the placement was wrong. Know what to watch for that goes beyond normal adjustment.

Relationship with the care team is not optional. Learn names, share what you know about your loved one, attend care plan meetings, and approach staff as partners. The family that is known and present is the family whose loved one receives better care.

Effective advocacy is specific, documented, and focused on outcomes. Start at the right level, escalate when needed, and know that your consistent presence is itself a form of protection.

Most placements work. When one does not, the same thinking that produced the original decision applies to the next one. Recognizing a bad fit and acting on it is advocacy, not failure.

ACTION STEP:

> *If a transition is approaching, use the next two weeks deliberately. Brief the care team on who your loved one is as a person, not just their diagnosis, but their history, their preferences, the things that bring them comfort. Prepare their room before they arrive. Plan move-in day with the same care you have given to every other step in this process. And if the transition has already happened and you are in the adjustment period, give it time, and use this chapter to help you know the difference between what is normal and what needs your attention.*

The transition is behind you. Chapter Ten, When Things Change, addresses what comes next in the longer arc: how to recognize when your loved one's care needs have shifted, how to handle changes in condition and level of care, and how to approach the conversations around end-of-life care with the same clarity and love that has guided every other decision in this process.

CHAPTER TEN

When Things Change

One of the things families are rarely told, but that professionals in this field know well — is that placement is not a final answer. It is a chapter. And like every chapter in a long story, it has an arc: a beginning defined by transition and adjustment, a middle shaped by routine and relationship, and eventually a shift, sometimes gradual, sometimes sudden, that signals the next thing is coming.

The nature of aging and serious illness is that things change. A person who enters an assisted living community with moderate needs may, over time, develop needs that exceed what that setting can safely provide. A person in a skilled nursing facility may decline significantly after a hospitalization, moving from a place of active rehabilitation toward one of comfort and presence. A person who seemed stable for months may shift suddenly, and everything the family thought they understood about what comes next needs to be reconsidered.

Families who have navigated placement once are not starting over when this happens. They have the tools. They know how to read signals, how to evaluate options, how to have hard conversations, how to advocate. What this chapter does is name the particular signals and transitions that belong to this later phase, including the ones that are hardest to look at directly: the shift toward end-of-life care, and what it means to hold your own grief while still showing up fully for the person you love.

> *Change inside a placement is not a failure of the placement. It is a feature of the underlying condition — of aging, of illness, of the human trajectory. Knowing how to recognize it, name it, and respond to it is the final form of advocacy this book asks of you.*

Recognizing When Care Needs Have Shifted

The signals that a person's care needs have changed are often familiar — they echo the signals that prompted the original placement decision. But they arrive in a different context, and they are sometimes harder to see clearly because the family has grown accustomed to the current situation. Stability, even imperfect stability, has a gravity. It is easier to recognize a change from outside than from inside a care arrangement that has become routine.

Physical and Clinical Signals

Watch for changes that represent a meaningful departure from the person's established baseline in the current setting. These include:

Increased frequency of falls or fall-related injuries, particularly if the current setting's protocols are not preventing them.

Significant or unexplained weight loss, which can signal declining appetite, difficulty swallowing, depression, or disease progression.

A hospitalization — particularly one that results in a meaningful functional decline from which the person does not fully recover.

New or worsening medical conditions that require a level of clinical monitoring or intervention the current setting is not equipped to provide.

Changes in pain management needs — increasing pain that is not being adequately addressed, or a shift in the nature of pain that suggests disease progression.

Cognitive and Behavioral Signals

For people living with dementia or other cognitive conditions, the progression of cognitive decline often brings changes that have direct implications for the appropriate level of care:

Increased wandering or elopement risk that the current setting cannot safely manage.

Significant behavioral changes — new or intensifying agitation, aggression, or sundowning, that are not being effectively addressed by the current care team's approach.

Loss of the ability to perform activities of daily living that the person was previously able to manage with minimal assistance.

A meaningful decline in communication ability, including the loss of speech or the ability to reliably express needs and discomfort.

What the Care Team Is Telling You

The care team is often the first to recognize when a person's needs have shifted beyond what the current setting can safely and appropriately address. If the nursing staff, the physician, or the social worker is raising concerns about the adequacy of the current level of care, or explicitly recommending a transition — take that seriously. They are not trying to move your loved one along. They are telling you something important about what they are seeing every day.

Ask direct questions. What specifically has changed? What does the current setting lack that the person now needs? What would the recommended next level of care provide? What is the timeline — is this urgent, or is there time to plan thoughtfully? The same clarity of information-gathering that served you in the original placement process serves you here.

Navigating a Change in Level of Care

When the signals are clear that a change is needed, families face a transition that in some ways resembles the original placement decision, and in some ways is different. The emotional weight may be heavier, because this transition often represents a meaningful marker of decline. The logistics may be more urgent, because changes in condition frequently happen faster than the original transition did. And the options may be more constrained, because the person's current condition narrows what settings can appropriately serve them.

Moving Within the Same Community

Many larger senior living communities are designed as continuing care environments — they include independent living, assisted living, memory care, and skilled nursing under one roof or campus. If your loved one is in such a community, a change in care level may mean a move within the same building rather than to a new facility entirely. This has real advantages: familiar staff, familiar physical environment, maintained social connections. Ask whether this option exists, what the transition process looks like, and whether there is a waitlist for the appropriate unit. If the move is likely in the future, it is worth getting on that list before it becomes urgent.

Moving to a New Setting

When the current setting cannot provide the needed level of care and a move to a new facility is required, the evaluation framework from Chapter Six still applies, but the timeline is often compressed and the stakes are higher. A few things worth knowing in this situation:

Hospital discharge planners and facility social workers are often the fastest route to identifying appropriate placements quickly. They know which facilities have beds, which specialize in the relevant conditions, and how to work through the referral process. Work with them, not around them.

The condition that requires the transition may qualify for Medicare-covered skilled nursing — particularly following a qualifying hospital stay. Revisit Chapter Five's guidance on Medicare coverage before assuming the financial picture has not changed.

If time allows even a brief evaluation of options, take it. A rushed placement that does not fit is harder to undo than one made with even a modest amount of information and care.

The adjustment process will begin again. Everything in Chapter Nine about the transition period applies to this move as well, and for people with cognitive impairment, subsequent moves often require particular care and attention to orientation and emotional continuity.

When the Setting Is Skilled Nursing and Needs Have Changed

For someone already in a skilled nursing facility, a significant change in condition may not require a move at all, but it does require a conversation. The care plan should be updated to reflect new needs. The goals of care, what the team is working toward and why, should be revisited. And if the person's condition has progressed to the point where aggressive intervention is no longer consistent with their wishes or their prognosis, the conversation about hospice and palliative care becomes essential.

The End-of-Life Conversation: Approaching It with Clarity and Love

There is no section of this book I want to write more carefully than this one. Not because the topic is taboo — I have spent 34 years sitting in rooms where this conversation needed to happen, and I have watched it go well and go badly, and I know what the difference looks like. I want to write it carefully because the families who have this conversation well are the ones who carry less regret. And reducing regret is, in the end, one of the things this book is for.

What Hospice and Palliative Care Actually Are

These two terms are often confused, and the confusion costs people access to care they could have had sooner.

Palliative care is specialized medical care focused on relief from the symptoms, pain, and stress of serious illness — at any stage of disease, alongside curative or life-prolonging treatment. It is not giving up. It is adding a layer of support focused on comfort and quality of life that curative treatment alone often does not provide. Any person with a serious illness can receive palliative care, and many should receive it much earlier than they do.

Hospice care is palliative care for people who are nearing the end of life — typically defined as a prognosis of six months or less if the illness runs its expected course. Electing hospice means shifting the goals of care from life prolongation to comfort, dignity, and quality of remaining life. It does not mean doing nothing. It means doing everything possible to ensure that the time remaining is as free from pain and distress as possible, and that the person and their family are supported through what comes next.

Hospice is covered by Medicare, Medicaid, and most private insurance. It can be provided in any care setting — in a skilled nursing facility, in an assisted living community, or at home. The hospice team comes to the person. It includes nursing, physician oversight, social work, chaplaincy, and bereavement support for the family. Most families who have used hospice say they wish they had elected it sooner. That is not a coincidence. It is a reflection of how much it provides and how long people wait before asking for it.

> *Hospice is not the end of care. It is a different kind of care, one organized entirely around comfort, dignity, and presence rather than treatment and intervention. For many people, and for many families, it is the most meaningful care their loved one receives.*

When to Have the Conversation

The conversation about end-of-life care goals — about what the person wants, what matters most to them, what they want to avoid — should happen before it is urgent. Ideally, it happens when the person can still participate in it fully. In practice, it often happens later than it should, because everyone is hoping the conversation will not be necessary yet. And then something shifts, and the conversation that could have been held thoughtfully needs to happen in a hospital room, or at a care conference, or in the middle of a crisis.

If you are reading this and your loved one is in a care setting and their condition is progressive, if you can see the arc of where things are going, even if the timeline is uncertain, the time to have this conversation is now. Not because it will resolve everything. Because it will make everything that follows clearer, more aligned with the person's wishes, and less weighted with regret.

What the Conversation Covers

A meaningful end-of-life conversation addresses several things, and it rarely happens all at once. It is a series of conversations, not a single talk:

Goals of care: What does the person want from their medical care at this stage? Are they willing to undergo hospitalization, resuscitation, or aggressive intervention if their condition worsens? Or is their priority comfort and presence over intervention and treatment?

Fears and wishes: What are they most afraid of? What do they most want — to be at home, to be without pain, to have family present, to have music playing? These specific, personal wishes are the ones that can actually be honored if they are spoken aloud and documented.

Practical documents: Does an advance directive exist? A POLST or MOLST form (Physician Orders for Life-Sustaining Treatment), which translates care wishes into physician orders that follow the person across care settings? A healthcare proxy who knows what the person wants and is prepared to advocate for it? These documents are the infrastructure that makes the conversation actionable.

The family: Who knows what? Are the people who need to understand the person's wishes informed? Is there alignment among family members about the direction of care, or are there disagreements that need to be surfaced and worked through before a crisis forces them?

How to Approach It

The principles from Chapter Seven, on how to have a hard conversation, apply here with full force. Start from love. Frame it as a conversation, not an announcement. Listen more than you speak. Let the person lead where they can. Acknowledge the weight of what you are talking about rather than trying to make it lighter than it is.

One thing that helps: naming the conversation directly. 'I want to talk with you about what you want, so that when things change I know how to be the advocate you deserve' is a different opening than 'We need to talk about what happens if things get worse.' The first centers the person's wishes and the relationship. The second centers the medical scenario. Both may arrive at the same place. But the first gets there more gently.

And for families where the person can no longer participate in this conversation, where cognitive decline or medical incapacity has closed that window, the same substituted judgment standard from Chapter Seven applies: what would this person have wanted, based on everything you know about them, the life they lived, and the values they held? That question is answerable. It may be painful to sit with, but it is answerable, and it is the most loving thing you can bring to the decision.

Supporting Yourself and Your Family Through Ongoing Loss

There is a particular kind of grief that belongs to long-term caregiving, one that is rarely named clearly and therefore rarely supported well. It is not the grief that comes after a death. It is the grief that comes before it, and alongside it: the accumulated losses of watching someone you love change, diminish, become less themselves, need more than they once did, remember less, recognize less, be present in ways that are different from the ways they once were. This is called anticipatory grief, and it is as real and as heavy as any other kind.

Naming the Loss as It Happens

One of the most useful things families can do is name what is being lost as it is being lost, not wait until after a death to grieve what has already changed. The parent who no longer recognizes you is a loss that happens before death and deserves to be mourned. The spouse whose personality has been altered by dementia is a loss that is happening now. Naming these losses — saying them aloud, to a therapist, a trusted friend, or another family member who is living the same thing — does not make them larger. It makes them more manageable. Grief unexpressed does not disappear. It accumulates and finds its way out in other forms.

What Families Need, and Often Do Not Ask For

Families in this phase need things that are often in short supply: permission to not be okay, reliable information about what to expect as conditions progress, time away from the caregiving role without guilt, and someone to talk to who understands the particular weight of this kind of love. These are not luxuries. They are the conditions under which sustained advocacy and presence become possible. A family member who is depleted cannot show up fully. A family member who has some support can.

Respite: Whether formal respite care, a temporary break from visiting, or simply an afternoon that is yours alone — taking time away is not abandonment. It is maintenance. The person you love needs you to still be standing.

Counseling and support groups: Caregiver support groups, including those specific to dementia, to cancer caregiving, to the experience of placing a loved one in long-term care — provide something that information alone cannot: the recognition that comes from being with people who understand what you are carrying. Ask the facility's social worker for local resources, or search through national organizations like the Caregiver Action Network, the Alzheimer's Association, or AARP's caregiver resources.

Honest conversations within the family: The grief of this phase is often carried unevenly across family members. One person may be more present to the loss; another may be protecting themselves through distance or denial. Finding moments to talk honestly, not only about logistics but about how you are actually doing — can prevent the compounded loss of relationships strained by what goes unspoken.

When the Death Comes

This book is not primarily a book about death. It is a book about the decisions that surround care — decisions made with love, under pressure, with incomplete information and full hearts. But the death of a person you have been caring for, and caring about — is the end of this arc, and it deserves a word.

When it comes, many families find that the grief is different from what they expected, sometimes smaller in the acute moment because so much has already been grieved, sometimes larger because the presence of the person, however changed, has been a constant. Both are true. Both are normal. What families consistently report is that the things they do not regret are the conversations they had, the time they spent present, the moments they chose love over logistics. And the things they do regret are almost always the things they waited too long to say or do.

You have been planning, advocating, showing up, and loving through one of the hardest things a person is asked to do. That will not be undone by death. It will be carried forward — in who you became through the process, in what you gave the person you love, and in the way you were present for them when they needed you most.

> *The goal of everything in this book has been the same from the first chapter to this one: to help you love someone well through a hard thing. You have done that. Whatever comes next, that is true.*

Key Takeaways from Chapter Ten

Placement is not a final answer. It is a chapter in a longer story. Knowing how to recognize when that chapter is ending, and what comes next — is the final form of advocacy this book asks of you.

The signals that care needs have shifted echo the original placement signals: physical decline, cognitive changes, hospitalizations with incomplete recovery, and explicit concerns from the care team. Take all of them seriously.

A change in level of care is a transition that calls on everything you have already learned. The timeline is often compressed; the approach is the same. Work with the care team, not around them.

Palliative care can and should begin earlier than most families request it. Hospice is a form of care — robust, covered, and organized entirely around comfort and dignity. Most families wish they had elected it sooner.

The end-of-life conversation should happen before it is urgent. It covers goals of care, fears and wishes, practical documents, and family alignment. It is a series of conversations, not a single talk, and it reduces regret more reliably than almost anything else you can do.

Anticipatory grief is real. Name what is being lost as it is being lost. Seek support. Take respite without guilt. The person you love needs you to still be standing.

The things families do not regret are the conversations they had and the time they spent present. Whatever logistics you have managed and whatever decisions you have made with love, that is what will remain.

ACTION STEP:

If your loved one is in a care setting, ask yourself honestly: are there signals of change you have been noticing but not naming? Is there a conversation about goals of care that should happen and has not yet? If the answer to either question is yes, use this chapter to prepare for what comes next. If you are earlier in the process, use it to understand the arc — so that when these moments arrive, you are not meeting them for the first time.

This chapter closes the practical section of this book. What follows is a final word, not a checklist or a framework, but a reflection on what this process asks of families, and what it gives back to those who move through it with intention, honesty, and love.

CLOSING

A Final Word

You picked up this book because someone you love needed more than you could give alone. Or because you could see what was coming and wanted to be ready. Or because a crisis had already arrived and you were trying to find your footing in the middle of it. Whatever brought you here, you came looking for help with one of the hardest things a person is asked to face, and you did the work. That matters. It matters more than you probably know.

I have spent years working with families at every stage of this process — before the decision, during it, and long after. And the thing I want to say to you, at the end of this book, is something that no checklist or chapter can fully convey: what you have done for the person you love is an act of profound devotion. Not the clean, uncomplicated kind that looks good from a distance, but the real kind. The kind that involves sitting with uncertainty and grief and exhaustion and still showing up. The kind that asks you to make hard decisions on behalf of someone you love, without the comfort of certainty, guided only by what you know and what you feel and what you believe they would want. That is not a small thing. That is everything.

The families who do this well, and you are among them, or you would not have read this far — share something that I have come to think of as a particular kind of courage. It is not the dramatic kind. It does not announce itself. It looks like calling the facility on a Tuesday morning to ask about a medication. It looks like having a conversation with a parent that neither of you wanted to have. It looks like driving to a memory care unit on a Thursday afternoon and sitting with someone who may not remember your name, and staying anyway, because you know that presence matters even when recognition does not. It looks like doing all of this while also living your own life, managing your own grief, and trying to take care of yourself well enough to keep going. That is the courage this journey requires. You have it.

I want to name a few things directly, as a closing gift of sorts — things I hope you will carry with you beyond this book.

You made the best decisions you could with the information you had. Not perfect decisions — there is no such thing in this territory. But thoughtful ones. Informed ones. Decisions made with love as the compass when the map ran out. If doubt revisits you, and it will, because that is the nature of caring deeply — come back to that. You did not choose carelessly. You chose with everything you had.

The grief you carry is not a sign that something went wrong. It is the shape that love takes when it meets loss. The two are not separate things. The grief is the love — redirected, transformed, made visible by the weight of what you have been through. It does not need to be fixed or finished. It needs to be honored.

Your loved one was fortunate to have you. Not because you did everything perfectly, no one does, but because you refused to do nothing. Because when the question arrived, you engaged with it. You sought information. You had conversations. You made decisions. You stayed present. Not every person who needs an advocate has one. Your loved one had you. That is not a small thing.

And finally: you are allowed to be proud of this. Not in the way that forgets the difficulty or papers over the grief, but in the quiet, solid way that comes from knowing you did something genuinely hard and genuinely important and did not look away from it. You showed up. Again and again, in all the forms that showing up required. That is worth something. It is worth more than I can say here.

> *Whatever chapter of this journey you are in — before the decision, inside it, or somewhere in the long arc that follows — I hope this book has given you something useful to hold. And I hope you know, with whatever certainty is available to you, that the love you brought to this was enough. It was always enough.*

With gratitude for the trust you have placed in these pages,

Cory Fosco

APPENDIX A

The When Readiness Checklist

This checklist is referenced throughout the book as a tool for tracking the signals that indicate a care transition may be approaching. It is not a scoring instrument — there is no threshold at which a specific number of checked boxes means the time has come. It is a mirror: a structured way of seeing clearly what is present across multiple domains at once. Complete it periodically, and look at it as a whole picture rather than a list of individual items.

SECTION 1: Safety

My loved one has fallen one or more times in the past six months.

My loved one has had a fall that resulted in injury.

My loved one has left the stove on, flooded the kitchen, or caused a household safety incident.

My loved one has gotten lost while driving or on foot in a familiar area.

My loved one is no longer able to manage medications reliably (missed doses, double doses, confusion about prescriptions).

My loved one lives alone and I am not confident they would be able to call for help in an emergency.

The home environment itself has become a safety concern (stairs, clutter, lack of grab bars, poor lighting).

SECTION 2: Physical Function

My loved one needs significant help with bathing, dressing, or personal hygiene.

My loved one is no longer able to prepare meals safely or reliably.

My loved one has experienced significant unintentional weight loss.

My loved one's mobility has declined to the point where they need assistance to walk safely.

My loved one has developed pressure wounds/injuries or skin integrity concerns related to limited mobility.

My loved one requires medical care (wound care, physical therapy, IV medications) that cannot be adequately managed at home.

SECTION 3: Cognitive Function

My loved one has a diagnosis of dementia, Alzheimer's disease, or mild cognitive impairment.

My loved one regularly forgets recent events, conversations, or appointments.

My loved one has become confused about time, place, or familiar people.

My loved one's judgment has declined — financial decisions, driving safety, inappropriate social behavior.

My loved one exhibits behavioral changes — increased agitation, aggression, paranoia, or withdrawal, that are difficult to manage.

My loved one is wandering or at risk of wandering.

SECTION 4: Caregiver Capacity

The primary caregiver is experiencing significant physical exhaustion.

The primary caregiver is experiencing anxiety, depression, or other mental health effects related to caregiving.

The primary caregiver has had to reduce or leave paid work to manage caregiving responsibilities.

The care needs now exceed what the primary caregiver can safely and consistently provide.

There is no backup caregiver available when the primary caregiver is unavailable.

The caregiving situation is causing serious strain on the caregiver's own relationships or health.

SECTION 5: Social and Emotional Wellbeing

My loved one has become notably isolated — fewer social connections, less engagement with activities they previously enjoyed.

My loved one has expressed loneliness or sadness about their current living situation.

My loved one's quality of life at home has declined in ways that a care community might address.

My loved one has expressed concern about being a burden on family members.

SECTION 6: Research and Planning

I have identified the type of care setting that appears to match my loved one's current needs.

I have researched facilities in the relevant geographic area.

I have toured at least one facility.

I have had a financial conversation, with a financial advisor or the facility's admissions team — about how care will be paid for.

Legal documents (healthcare proxy, durable power of attorney, advance directive) are in place.

The relevant family members have had at least one substantive conversation about the care planning situation.

A concentration of checked boxes in any single section warrants attention. Multiple checked boxes across three or more sections is a strong indicator that a transition conversation, with the care team, with the family, or with a professional — is overdue.

APPENDIX B

Questions to Ask on a Facility Tour

These questions are drawn from Chapter Six. Not every question will be relevant to every facility or every situation — use them as a starting point and adapt them to what matters most for your loved one. Bring this list. Take notes. Compare your notes across facilities when you are making the final decision.

About Staffing

What is the staff-to-resident ratio during the day? In the evening? Overnight?

What is the staff turnover rate? How does it compare to the state or national average?

Are staff members employees of the facility, or contracted through an agency?

What training do direct care staff receive? How often is it updated?

Is there a consistent assignment model — meaning residents are cared for by the same aides regularly?

Who is the medical director, and how often are they on site?

Is there a registered nurse on site 24 hours a day, or on call?

About Daily Life and Culture

Can you describe a typical day for a resident in this unit?

What does the activity calendar look like? How many programs are offered per week?

What options do residents have for meals — timing, menu choices, dining location?

How does the facility accommodate individual preferences and routines?

What does the facility do to help new residents adjust during the first weeks?

How are residents who prefer to stay in their rooms kept engaged and connected?

About Safety and Care Quality

What is the facility's most recent state inspection report, and how can I access it?

What is the facility's star rating on Medicare's Care Compare, and how has it trended?

How does the facility handle medical emergencies?

What is the fall prevention protocol?

How are behavioral concerns, particularly for residents with dementia, managed?

What is the process for notifying families about changes in a resident's condition?

About Family Involvement

How does the facility communicate with families on a regular basis?

Does the facility have a family portal or digital communication tool?

When are care plan meetings held, and how are families involved?

What is the process for raising a concern or complaint?

Is there a family or resident council, and how active is it?

About Finances and Admission

What is included in the base monthly rate, and what costs extra?

How often do rates increase, and by how much historically?

What is the facility's policy on Medicaid — do you accept it, and what is the process if a resident's private funds are exhausted?

What is the discharge policy if care needs exceed what the facility can provide?

What are the terms of the admissions agreement regarding deposits and refunds?

What to Observe — Beyond the Questions

Do residents appear clean, well-groomed, and appropriately dressed?

Are residents engaged and moving around, or largely confined to their rooms?

How do staff interact with residents — warmth, eye contact, using their names?

Does the facility smell clean throughout, including in resident rooms and hallways?

Is the physical environment well-maintained, with functional equipment and clean common spaces?

How does the staff respond to you as a visitor — welcoming, transparent, willing to answer questions?

APPENDIX C

Glossary of Care Setting Types

Long-term care involves a range of settings that are frequently confused or conflated. This glossary provides plain-language descriptions of the most common options. For a fuller discussion of how to evaluate which setting is right for your loved one, see Chapter One.

Independent Living (IL)

A residential community designed for older adults who are largely self-sufficient but want the convenience, social connection, and amenities of a community setting. Independent living typically includes housing (apartments or cottages), meals, housekeeping, transportation, and programming, but does not include personal care or medical services. Also called senior living, retirement community, or 55+ community.

Assisted Living (AL)

A residential care setting that provides support with activities of daily living (bathing, dressing, medication management) while maintaining a homelike environment. Assisted living is regulated at the state level, so services and licensing requirements vary widely. Most assisted living communities serve residents who need some help but do not require 24-hour skilled nursing care.

Memory Care

A specialized care setting, either a standalone community or a dedicated unit within a larger facility — designed for people with Alzheimer's disease, dementia, or other cognitive impairments. Memory care environments are typically secured to prevent wandering, staffed by personnel with specialized dementia training, and programmed with activities designed for people with cognitive decline.

Skilled Nursing Facility (SNF)

A licensed facility that provides 24-hour nursing care, rehabilitation services (physical, occupational, and speech therapy), and medical management for people with complex or ongoing clinical needs. SNFs serve both short-term rehabilitation patients (recovering from a hospitalization or surgery) and long-term residents who require ongoing nursing care. Also called a nursing home or nursing facility.

Continuing Care Retirement Community (CCRC)

A campus or community that offers multiple levels of care — typically independent living, assisted living, memory care, and skilled nursing — on the same site. CCRCs allow residents to move between levels of care as their needs change without leaving the campus. They typically require a large entrance fee and monthly fees, and are governed by contracts (Type A, B, or C) that define the terms of care and financial arrangements. Also called a Life Plan Community.

Long-Term Acute Care Hospital (LTACH)

A specialized hospital setting that provides intensive medical care for patients with serious, complex conditions who require a longer period of acute-level treatment than a typical hospital stay allows. Unlike a skilled nursing facility, an LTACH provides hospital-level care, including ventilator weaning, wound care, and complex rehabilitation — typically for patients who are medically stable but not yet ready for a lower level of care. LTACH length of stays average 25 days or more. Medicare covers LTACH care under specific criteria. Not all markets have LTACH facilities available.

Residential Care Home / Board and Care

A small, home-based setting — typically a private residence, that provides personal care and supervision for a small number of residents (often six or fewer). Residential care homes can offer a more intimate, family-like environment than larger facilities, and may be appropriate for individuals who are uncomfortable in institutional settings. Quality and licensure vary significantly by state.

Home Health Care

Medical or therapeutic services provided in a person's home by licensed professionals — registered nurses, physical therapists, occupational therapists, speech therapists, or medical social workers. Home health care is typically prescribed by a physician and may be covered by Medicare or insurance for qualifying conditions. It is distinct from home care (non-medical personal assistance) and private-duty nursing.

Hospice

A philosophy and program of care for people who are approaching the end of life — generally defined as a prognosis of six months or less if the illness follows its expected course. Hospice focuses on comfort, quality of life, and support for the patient and family rather than curative treatment. It can be provided in any setting — home, nursing facility, assisted living, or a dedicated hospice residence. Hospice is a Medicare benefit and is also covered by most Medicaid and private insurance plans.

Palliative Care

Specialized medical care focused on relief from pain, symptoms, and the stress of serious illness. Unlike hospice, palliative care can be provided at any stage of illness and alongside curative treatment. It is provided by a team of specialists — physicians, nurses, social workers, and chaplains — working in concert with the patient's primary care and specialist providers. Palliative care is not about giving up. It is about ensuring quality of life throughout the illness journey.

APPENDIX D

Glossary of Key Terms

The following terms appear throughout this book and in conversations with care providers, facilities, and financial and legal professionals. Understanding them will help you approach those conversations with greater confidence.

Activities of Daily Living (ADLs)

The basic self-care tasks a person performs daily: bathing, dressing, grooming, toileting, transferring (moving from bed to chair, etc.), and eating. ADLs are used to assess functional capacity and determine appropriate level of care. Related: Instrumental Activities of Daily Living (IADLs) — more complex tasks such as managing medications, preparing meals, managing finances, and driving.

Advance Directive

A legal document that expresses a person's wishes regarding medical treatment in the event they become unable to make or communicate decisions. Common forms include a living will (specific treatment preferences), a healthcare proxy or healthcare power of attorney (designating someone to make decisions on your behalf), and a POLST (Physician Orders for Life-Sustaining Treatment).

Bed Hold

A policy that allows a resident's bed at a facility to be held for them during a hospital stay or temporary absence. Medicaid and private pay policies differ on how long a bed hold lasts and whether it is covered. Clarifying this policy before a hospitalization is important.

Care Plan

A written document, developed collaboratively by the care team and family, that outlines a resident's current needs, goals, and the specific services and interventions to be provided. Care plans are reviewed and updated at regular intervals and at any significant change in condition. Families have the right to participate in care plan meetings.

Cognitive Impairment

A broad term for conditions that affect memory, thinking, judgment, language, or other cognitive functions. Mild cognitive impairment (MCI) involves changes that are noticeable but do not significantly interfere with daily functioning. Dementia refers to a more severe decline that affects the ability to perform daily activities. Alzheimer's disease is the most common form of dementia.

Discharge Planner

A hospital employee, typically a social worker or nurse, whose role is to coordinate a patient's transition from the hospital to the next care setting. Discharge planners work under time pressure and may not have detailed knowledge of specific facilities. Families who have done advance research are better positioned to participate meaningfully in discharge planning conversations.

Durable Power of Attorney for Healthcare (DPOA-HC)

A legal document designating a specific person (the healthcare proxy or agent) to make medical decisions on behalf of the individual if they become unable to make or communicate those decisions. Distinct from a financial power of attorney. Both should be in place and accessible.

Geriatric Care Manager (GCM)

A licensed professional — typically a social worker or nurse, who specializes in the needs of older adults and their families. GCMs can conduct assessments, develop care plans, coordinate services, evaluate facility options, and serve as family advocates and navigators. Also called an aging life care professional.

Long-Term Care Ombudsman

An independent advocate, designated under federal law, whose role is to investigate complaints and protect the rights of residents in nursing homes, assisted living facilities, and other long-term care settings. Every state has an ombudsman program. Services are free and confidential.

Medicaid

A joint federal and state program that provides health coverage, including long-term care benefits, to individuals who meet income and asset eligibility requirements. Medicaid is the primary payer for long-term care in the United States. Eligibility rules, covered services, and facility participation vary widely by state.

Medicare

The federal health insurance program for people 65 and older and certain younger people with disabilities. Medicare covers skilled nursing facility care on a limited, time-defined basis following a qualifying hospital stay, but does not cover ongoing custodial care (help with ADLs) in a nursing home or assisted living facility. Understanding this distinction is essential for financial planning.

POLST (Physician Orders for Life-Sustaining Treatment)

A medical order — distinct from an advance directive, that documents specific treatment preferences (resuscitation, hospitalization, artificial nutrition) in a portable form that follows the patient across care settings. A POLST is signed by a physician and is immediately actionable by emergency responders and care providers. Also known as MOLST, MOST, or POST in some states.

Spend-Down

The process by which a person depletes their assets to the Medicaid eligibility threshold before qualifying for Medicaid coverage of long-term care. Medicaid has strict rules about asset transfers and look-back periods. Consulting an elder law attorney before major asset transfers is strongly advised.

Substituted Judgment

A standard used in medical decision-making when a person lacks the capacity to make their own decisions. Substituted judgment asks: what would this person have decided, based on their known values, preferences, and prior statements? It is preferred over a 'best interest' standard when enough is known about the person to apply it meaningfully.

APPENDIX E

Resources and Organizations

The following organizations provide information, support, and advocacy for older adults, family caregivers, and those facing long-term care decisions. This list is not exhaustive — it is a starting point. Many of these organizations offer free resources, helplines, and referral services.

Federal Government Resources

Medicare.gov — Official Medicare information, including the Nursing Home Compare and Care Compare tools for researching facility quality ratings, inspection reports, and staffing data. medicare.gov

Medicaid.gov — Information on Medicaid eligibility, covered services, and state-by-state program details. medicaid.gov

Benefits.gov — A federal resource for identifying government benefits programs available to older adults and caregivers. benefits.gov eldercare.acl.gov — The Eldercare Locator, a public service of the U.S. Administration on Aging that connects older adults and caregivers to local services and resources. 1-800-677-1116.

Care Navigation and Advocacy

Aging Life Care Association (ALCA) — The professional association for geriatric care managers and aging life care professionals. Includes a searchable directory for finding a professional in your area. aginglifecare.org

Long-Term Care Ombudsman Program — Every state has an ombudsman program that advocates for residents in long-term care facilities. Contact your state's program through the Eldercare Locator or the National Long-Term Care Ombudsman Resource Center at ltcombudsman.org

National Alliance for Caregiving — Research and resources for family caregivers, including guides to working through the care system. caregiving.org

Dementia and Memory Care

Lewy Body Dementia Association — Information and support specifically for families navigating Lewy body dementia. lbda.org

Association for Frontotemporal Degeneration — Support and resources for families dealing with frontotemporal dementia. theaftd.org

Financial and Legal Planning

National Academy of Elder Law Attorneys (NAELA) — A professional association for attorneys specializing in elder law and special needs planning. Includes a searchable directory. naela.org

National Council on Aging (NCOA) — Resources on benefits enrollment, financial assistance programs, and the

BenefitsCheckUp tool for identifying programs your loved one may qualify for. ncoa.org

American Association for Long-Term Care Insurance — Information on long-term care insurance products and planning. aaltci.org

Caregiver Support

Well Spouse Association — Support specifically for spousal caregivers, including in-person support groups and a newsletter. wellspouse.org

Hospice and Palliative Care

Get Palliative Care — Clear, accessible information about palliative care for patients and families, including how to request a consultation. getpalliativecare.org

Compassion & Choices — Resources and advocacy on end-of-life options and advance care planning. compassionandchoices.org

URLs and contact information are current as of the manuscript preparation date and should be verified before publication.

About the Author

Cory Fosco has spent over three decades working at the intersection of long-term care, healthcare technology, and the families facing some of the most difficult decisions of their lives.

His career in elder care began where the best ones often do, not in a boardroom, but on the ground. After graduating from Loyola University Chicago, he accepted a full-time volunteer position with the Jesuit Volunteer Corps, working as an outreach worker for a senior center in Mesa, Arizona. That experience — learning to identify what older adults needed, providing the resources to meet those needs, and above all, caring — set the course for everything that followed.

He went on to serve as a Social Worker and Director of Admissions at two skilled nursing facilities in Phoenix, and later as Director of Admissions and Market Development Manager for HCR ManorCare. Those years working directly with residents, families, and care teams gave him a perspective on this work that no amount of time in an executive suite can replicate.

From there, Fosco moved into healthcare technology. He served in senior executive roles at ECIN and Resource Systems before joining PointClickCare in 2017, where he currently serves as Vice President of Enterprise Sales. PointClickCare is the most widely used cloud-based technology platform in skilled nursing and senior living in North America.

Parallel to his professional life, Fosco earned a Master of Arts in Creative Nonfiction from Northwestern University and spent nearly a decade teaching writing at the community college level.

His short fiction, creative nonfiction, and poetry have appeared in numerous literary magazines.

His chapbook, *Empty Streets,* was published by Alien Buddha Press in June 2024.

Fosco serves on the advisory board of Disability Rights Advocates and has volunteered with Second Sense and Guide Dogs for the Blind, including teaching creative writing in support of the blind and vision-impaired community, a cause close to his heart through his wife, Cyndi, who is vision impaired and an active advocate in the blind community.

He lives in the Chicago area.